STAR WARS

PANEL TO PANEL

VOLUME 2

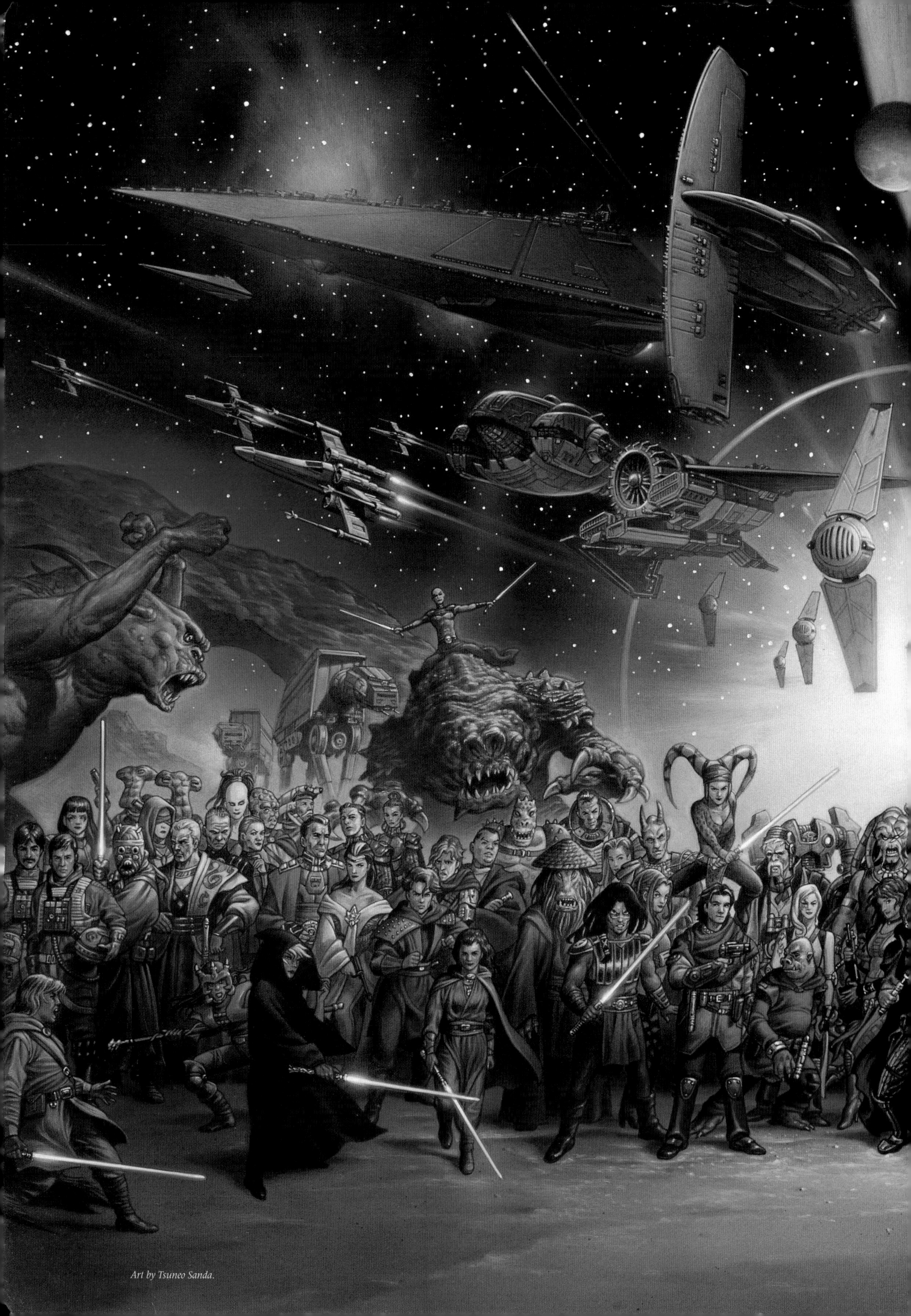

Art by Tsuneo Sanda.

STAR WARS®

PANEL TO PANEL

VOLUME 2

EXPANDING THE UNIVERSE

TEXT BY
RANDY STRADLEY

DARK HORSE BOOKS®

TSUNEO SANDA

publisher
MIKE RICHARDSON

designer
TONY ONG

art director
LIA RIBACCHI

assisting editors
DAVE MARSHALL
JEREMY BARLOW

editor
RANDY STRADLEY

The editor gratefully acknowledges the assistance of Elaine Mederer, Jann Moorhead, David Anderman, Leland Chee, Sue Rostoni, and Amy Gary at Lucas Licensing.

Star Wars®: Panel to Panel Volume 2

Published by Dark Horse Books, a division of Dark Horse Comics, Inc.

www.darkhorse.com
www.starwars.com

To find a comics shop in your area, call the Comic Shop Locator Service
toll-free at 1-888-266-4226

First edition: May 2007

ISBN-10: 1-59307-793-9
ISBN-13: 978-1-59307-793-8

1 3 5 7 9 10 8 6 4 2
Printed in China

TABLE OF CONTENTS

A WORD ABOUT THE CONTENTS

Three years ago, when I wrote the introduction to the first *Star Wars: Panel to Panel* book, I commented on how, due to space limitations, many of the images I had wanted to include in that volume had to be left out. But I allowed that if that volume was successful, we might someday be able to produce a second. "Someday" came sooner than I imagined! I won't bore you with another recitation of the deliberations that went into deciding which images to use in this book, and which to set aside. Suffice to say, I *still* did not have space to include all that I wanted.

As with the first volume, the artist(s) for each illustration, and the comic book in which the piece was first published and (where applicable) in which graphic novel collection it can currently be seen are indicated. Where story pages are reproduced, the writers have also been credited.

For those readers curious to know exactly when and where certain stories take place, or for those interested in further exploring the rich galaxy of *Star Wars* comics and graphic novels, a *Star Wars* timeline and galaxy map are included at the end of this book.

Randy Stradley
October 2006

THE OLD, OLD REPUBLIC

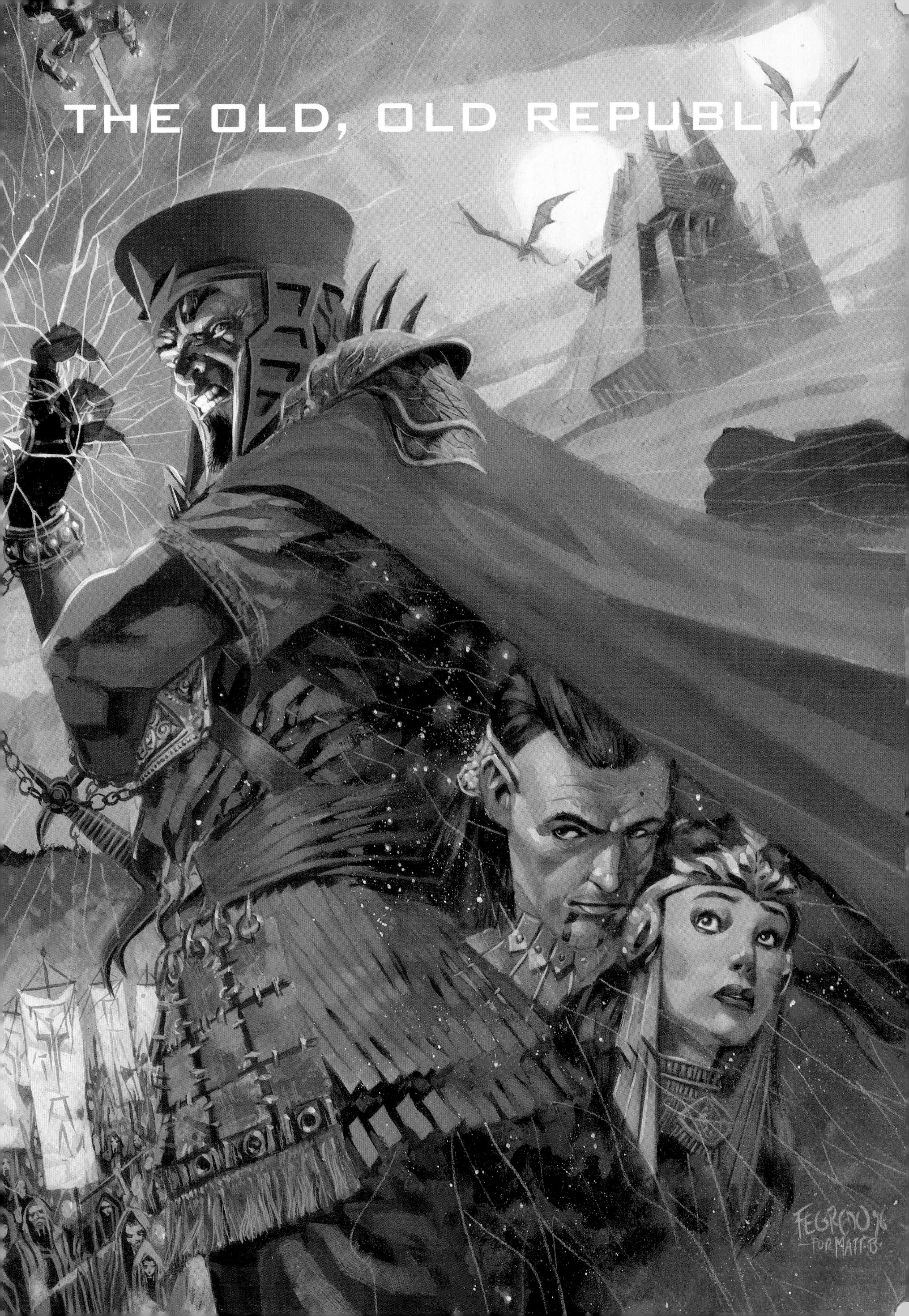

THE COMING OF THE SITH

As of this writing, Dark Horse's earliest entry on the *Star Wars* timeline begins approximately five thousand years before the Battle of Yavin—the climax of the film *Star Wars*: Episode IV—*A New Hope*. Admittedly, this is a good deal further back than "a long time ago," but it is a relatively recent point in the history of the "galaxy far, far away." Obi-Wan Kenobi gave us a clue to just how far back things began when he said, "The Jedi were the guardians of the Republic for a thousand generations." A generation is typically regarded as about twenty to twenty-five years. Twenty times a thousand. That *is* a long time ago!

Previous page: art by Duncan Fegredo, Tales of the Jedi: The Golden Age of the Sith *collection (1997).*

If you've seen the films, you know that there are ever only two Sith at one time—master and apprentice. But it wasn't always so. When two explorers in search of a new hyperspace route ended up on the planet Korriban, they discovered not just two Sith, but an entire Sith empire!

Art by Christopher Moeller. Tales of the Jedi: Golden Age of the Sith #0 (1996).

Exiled following an ancient schism, a group of Jedi who had succumbed to the dark side conquered Korriban and its native species, the Sith, who eventually lent their name to the dark religion. After becoming the Dark Lord of the Sith, Naga Sadow unleashed his armies on the unsuspecting worlds of the Republic.

As they had for millennia, the Jedi defended the Republic, and Naga Sadow was defeated.

In those far-flung days, it was common practice for Jedi to marry and raise children. (Translation: the Prequel Trilogy of films had not yet been written, and writers didn't know any better.) When Jedi Andur Sunrider was killed by the agents of an evil Hutt, his wife Nomi took up her husband's lightsaber and eventually became one of the great Jedi of the era.

This page and opposite: art by Dave Dorman. Tales of the Jedi #3 (1993) *and* Tales of the Jedi #5 (1994). *This series was collected under the subtitle* Knights of the Old Republic, *a title that has since been resurrected, both for a series of video games set during the same era, and for a new comic book series launched in 2006.*

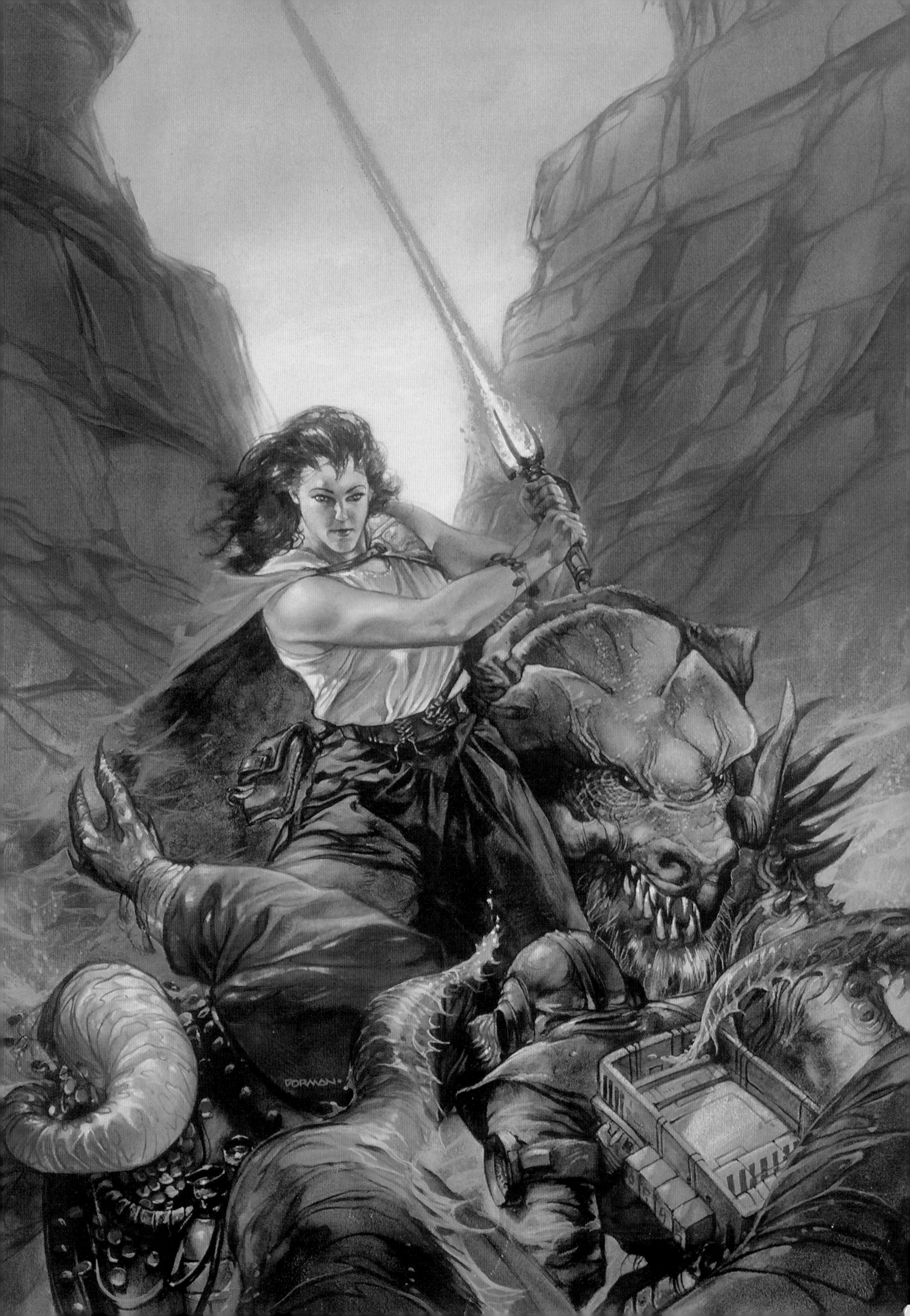
DORMAN

But though their empire was destroyed, the idea of the Sith had taken root in the galaxy, and just over a thousand years after Naga Sadow's demise, a new wave of Jedi felt the lure of the dark side. The Republic was once again at war . . .

. . . pitting Jedi against Jedi, and brother against brother—in this case fallen Jedi Ulic Qel-Droma and his bother Cay. And even when the war was over, peace did not mean safety. On the following pages, Twi'lek Jedi Tott Doneeta faces a heat storm on his native Ryloth.

Art by Hugh Fleming. Tales of the Jedi: The Sith War *#5 (1995). Following pages: script by Kevin J. Anderson, art by Chris Gossett, colored by Dave Nestelle, lettering by Willie Schubert.* Tales of the Jedi: Redemption *#1 (1998), collected in 2001.*

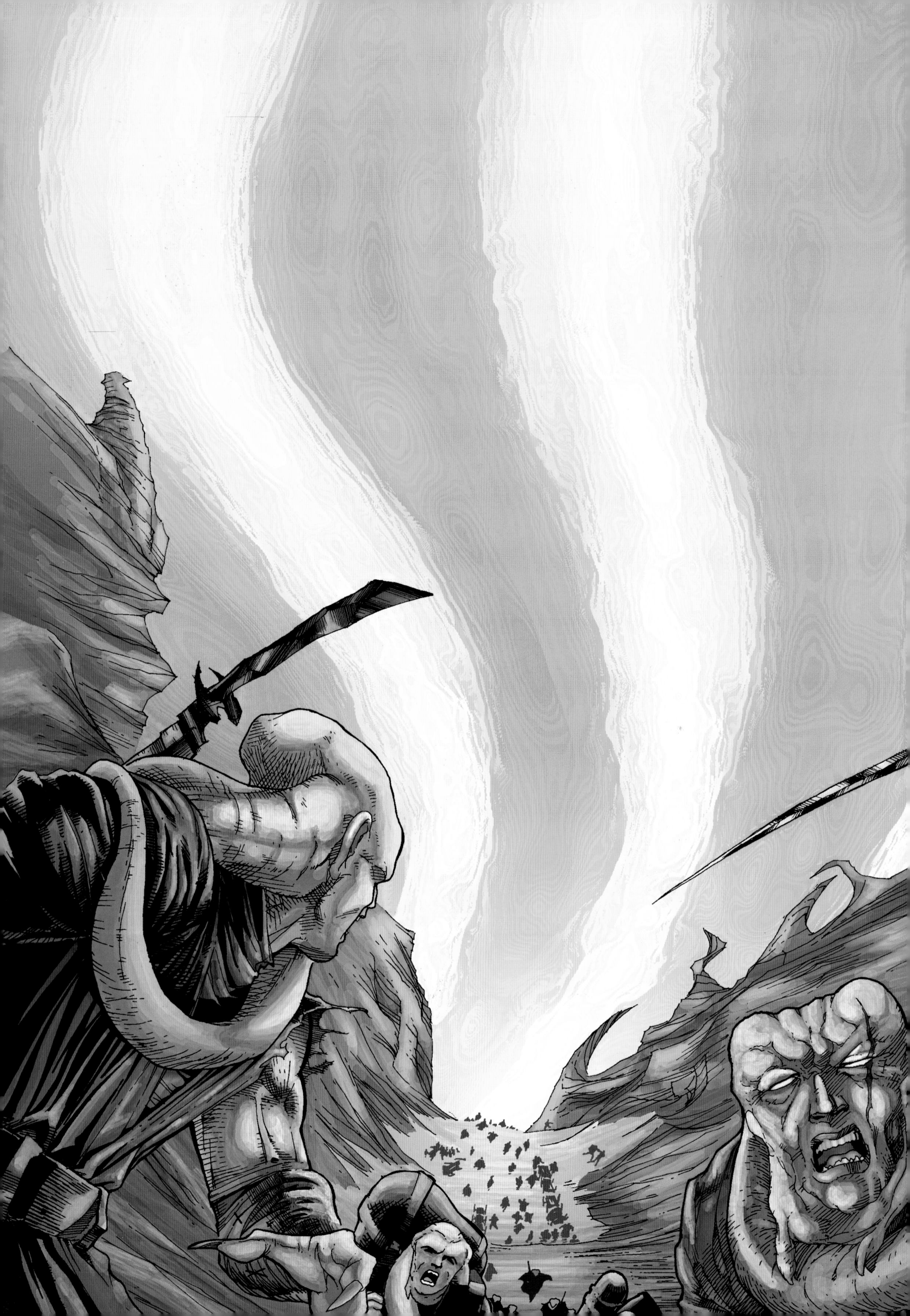

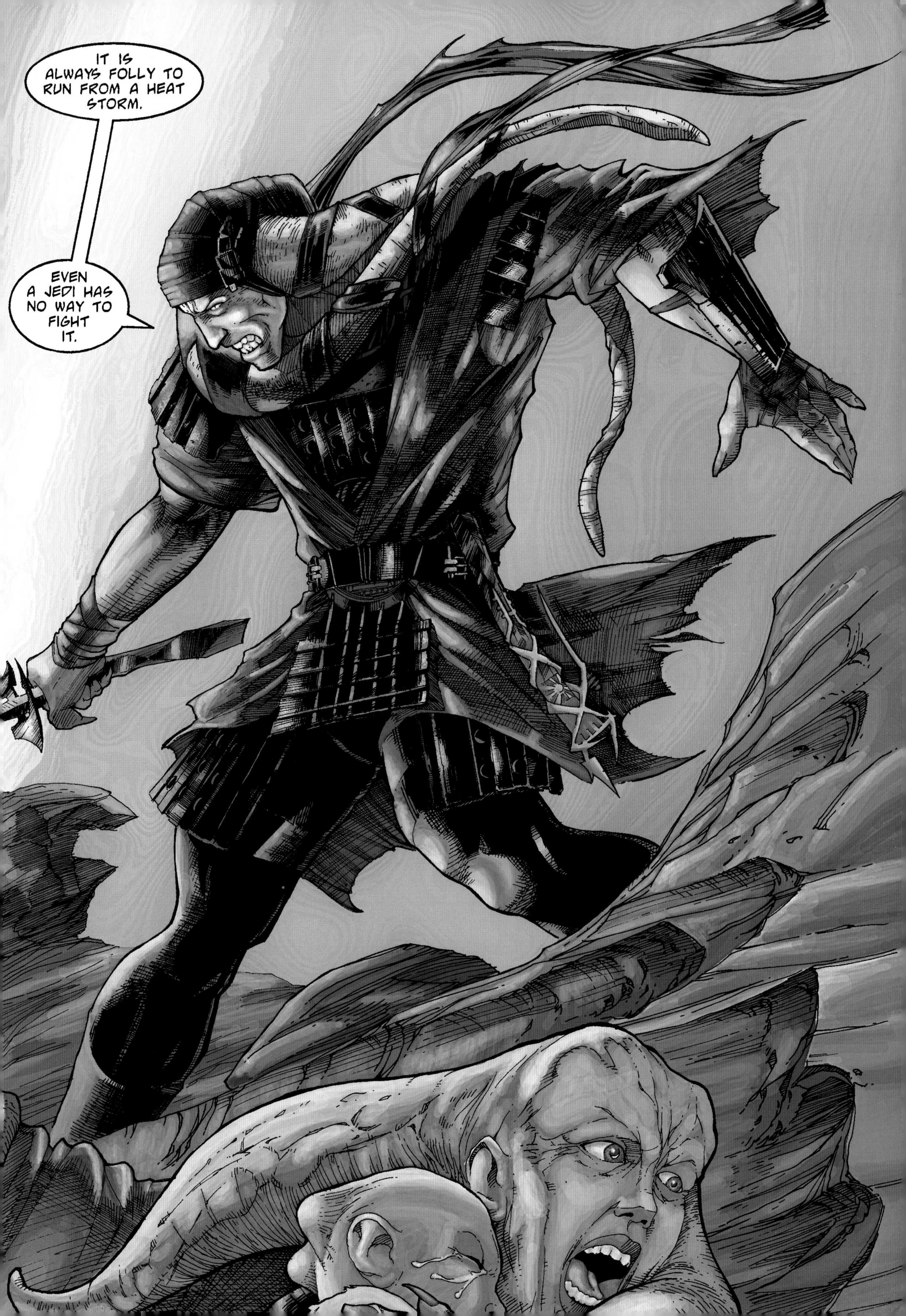
IT IS ALWAYS FOLLY TO RUN FROM A HEAT STORM.
EVEN A JEDI HAS NO WAY TO FIGHT IT.

That which does not kill you, Tott Doneeta, makes you stronger. You hope.

Art by Igor Kordey. Tales of the Jedi: Redemption #2 *(1998).*

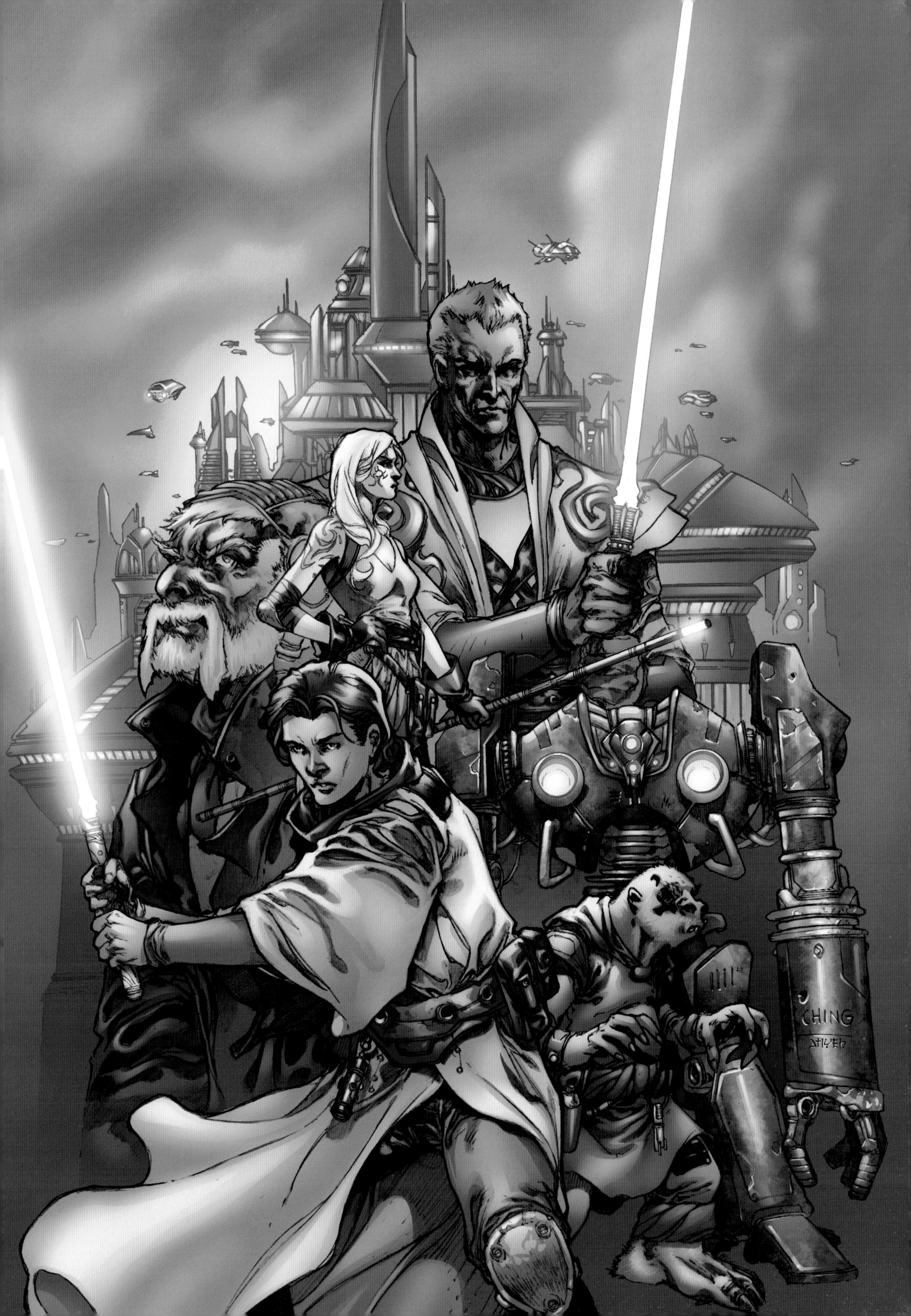
CHING

KNIGHTS AND KNAVES

By 2001, after chronicling the beginnings of the Jedi-Sith conflict over the course of seven graphic novels, we at Dark Horse turned our attention to other periods along the *Star Wars* timeline. Then, in 2003, LucasArts released the video game *Knights of the Old Republic*, set approximately one generation after the Sith War. So successful was the game that a sequel followed a year later. In planning a revamp of their *Star Wars* line for Dark Horse's twentieth anniversary, Dark Horse editors decided to return to the era of the Old Republic and introduce a new set of characters who, while caught up in the sweeping events of the time, had their own problems and own agendas.

Previous page: art by Brian Ching, colored by Michael Atiyeh. Knights of the Old Republic #0 (2006).

Depending on how you look at it, Zayne Carrick is either the unluckiest Padawan (student Jedi) of all time, or the luckiest. Clumsy and barely sufficient in his studies and abilities, Zayne was late for his own graduation to Knighthood—a ceremony in which all of his fellow students were killed.

Art by Travis Charest. Knights of the Old Republic #1 (2006).

21

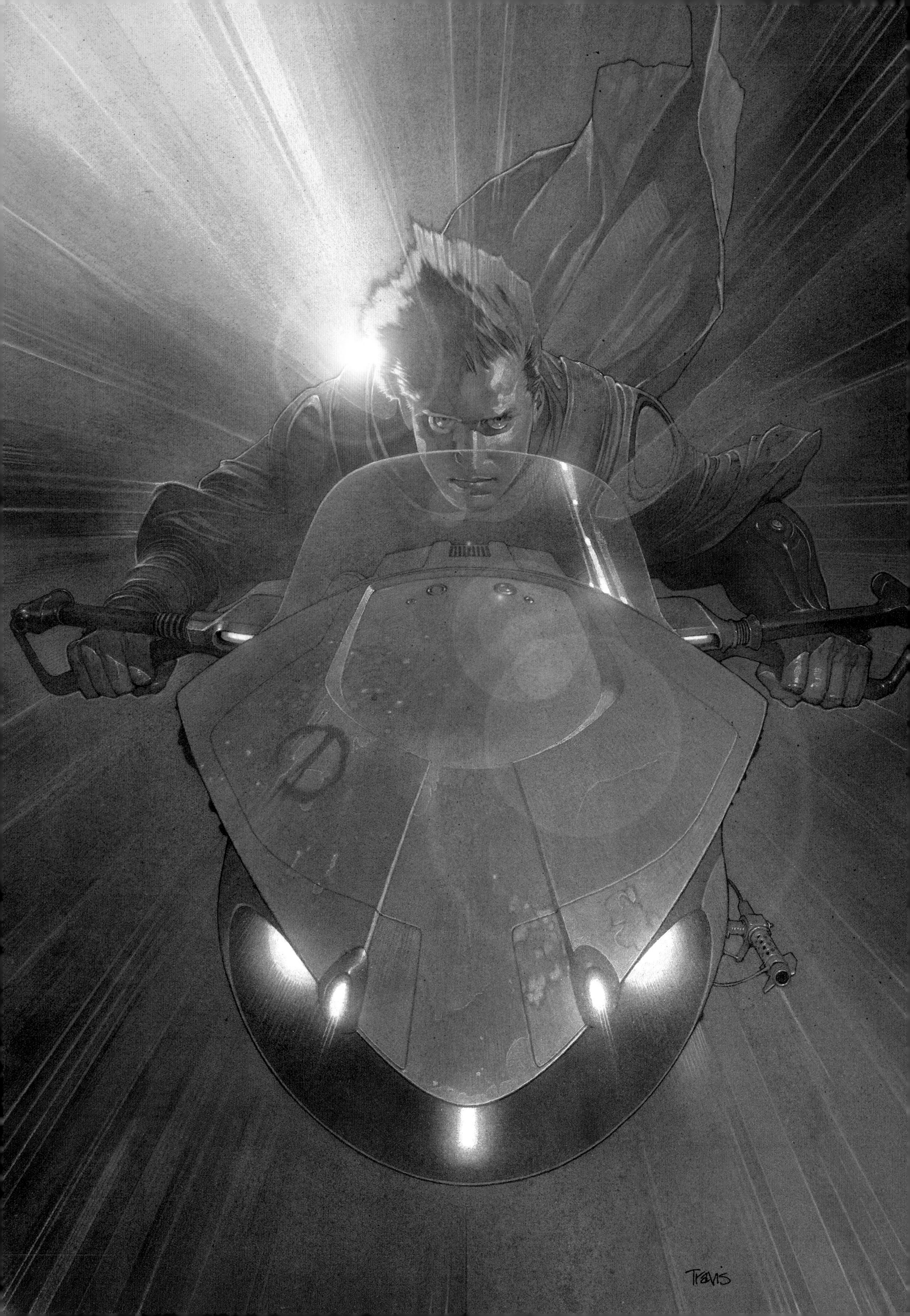
TRAVIS

Framed by his own Master for the murders of his classmates, Zayne went on the lam. Pursued by local authorities and the Jedi, Carrick fell in with thieves, smugglers, and other wanted outlaws . . . which didn't help his claims of innocence.

Both pages: art by Travis Charest. Knights of the Old Republic #2 and #4 (2006).

23

Zayne's bad luck held in his choice of criminal associates: (from left to right) Jarael, Marn "Gryph" Hierogryph, and Camper at the controls. Their escape vehicle, the *Last Resort*, turned out to be no more reliable than Han Solo's *Millennium Falcon*.

Script by John Jackson Miller, art by Brian Ching, colored by Michael Atiyeh, lettering by Michael Heisler. Knights of the Old Republic #3 (2006), *collected in* Knights of the Old Republic *Volume 1 (2007).*

Even with the addition of often-necessary droid "muscle" in the form of hybrid loader droid T1-LB ("Elbee"), bad luck seemed to follow Zayne and his companions no matter where they went . . .

Script by John Jackson Miller, art by Dustin Weaver, colored by Michael Atiyeh, lettering by Michael Heisler. Knights of the Old Republic #8 (2006)

. . . and where they went was into the heart of the Mandalorian War. "Manda-who-ians?" you ask? Well, the Mandalorians were never mentioned in the films, but somewhere along the line it was established in the "Expanded Universe" that Boba Fett wears Mandalorian armor, and that he was the last surviving Madalorian warrior in the galaxy.

THE MANDALORIANS ARE ATTACKING -- FOR REAL!

Then along came *Attack of the Clones*, and the origin of Boba's progenitor Jango (not his dad, because Boba is a clone, remember) was quickly reassessed. In the meantime, however, the Mandalorians had been given a backstory in Dark Horse's *Sith War* comics and LucasArts' *Knights of the Old Republic* games. And, if one Mandalorian was good, thousands must be better. Suffice to say, the mercenary soldiers now populate practically every era of the *Star Wars* timeline.

If being chased by the Republic military, the Mandalorian super-commandos, and a rogue Jedi cabal weren't enough, Zayne's new traveling companions—particularly the addled inventor Camper and his protector Jarael—weren't exactly thrilled to have him aboard, blaming the hapless Padawan for the fresh set of problems that plagued them.

But Zayne's biggest challenge remained clearing his name—and discovering the identity of a space-suited figure who, a Jedi vision said, would topple the Jedi order.

Art by Travis Charest. Knights of the Old Republic #5 (2006).

29

Unfortunately, that space-suited figure might just turn out to be *him*. (In this flashback scene, Zayne and his fellow Padawans are deposited on a dangerous moon as part of their Jedi training.)

Script by John Jackson Miller, art by Brian Ching, colored by Michael Atiyeh, lettering by Michael Heisler. Knights of the Old Republic #3 *(2006).*

But with nearly three thousand years separating his adventures from the next major landmark along the timeline, Zayne and his pals have time to accomplish their goals. And they may *need* that time to deal with threats like the bounty-hunting Ithorian siblings, the Moomo Brothers (above).

This page: art by HOON. Knights of the Old Republic #11 (2006). *Opposite: art by Travis Charest.* Knights of the Old Republic #6 (2006).

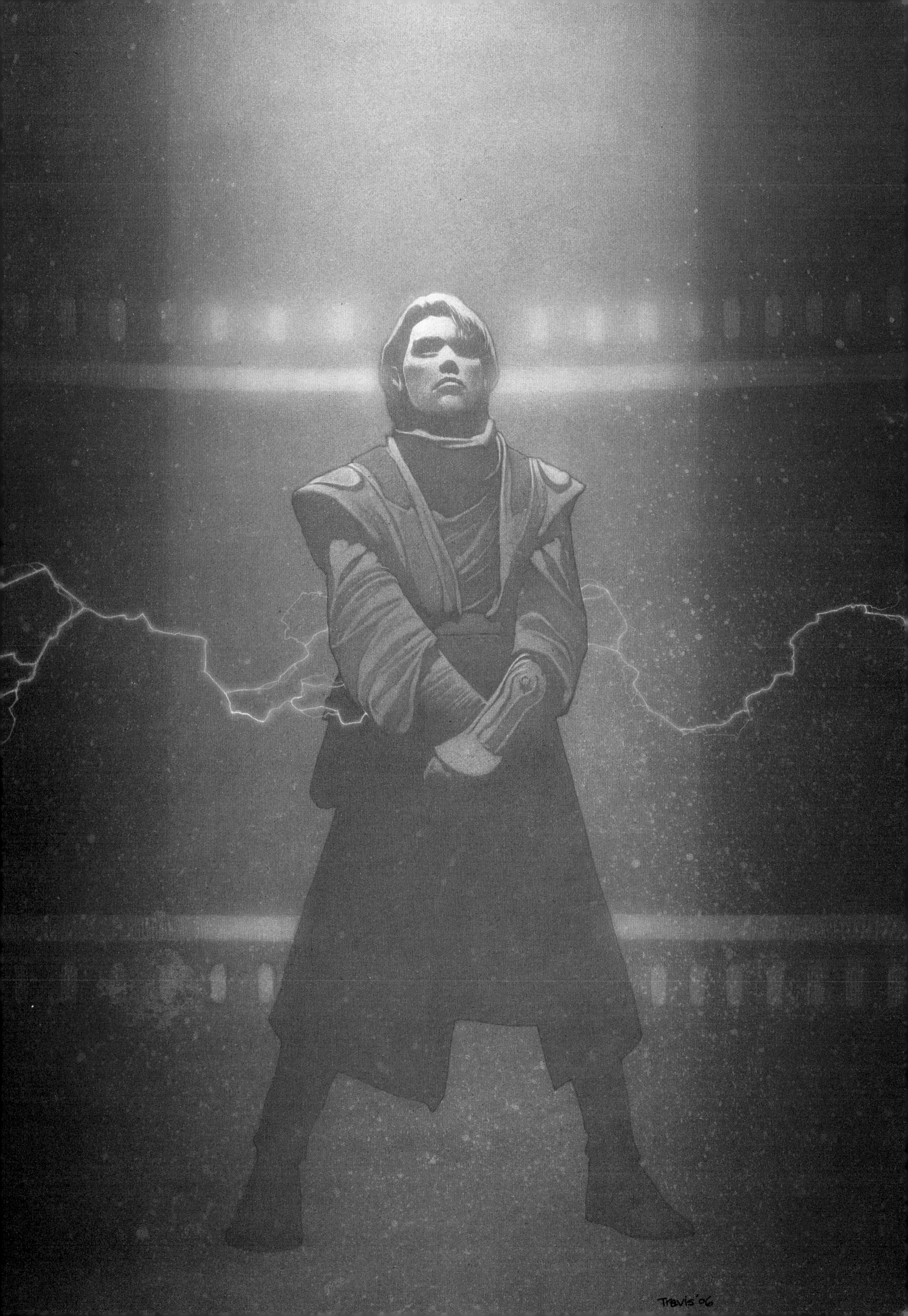
Travis '06

Some 2964 years after Zayne Carrick's adventures began, there came a turning point in the history of the galaxy. For nearly four thousand years the Sith Empire had been at war—on and off—with the Jedi and the Republic. One thousand years before the Battle of Yavin (1000 BBY), things finally came to a head between the two on the planet Ruusan. The Jedi Army of Light and the Sith Brotherhood of Darkness met in a series of fateful battles.

Art by Andrew Robinson, colored by Dave Stewart. Jedi Vs. Sith #1 (2001). Also appears in the collection of the same name (2002).

In the seventh and final battle the Sith Lords, cornered and divided against themselves, unleashed a suicide weapon that destroyed nearly every Force-user on the planet—Jedi and Sith alike.

Script by Darko Macan, pencils by Ramon F. Bachs, inks by Raul Fernandez, colored by Chris Blythe, lettering by Steve Dutro. Jedi vs. Sith #4 (2001), and the collection (2002).

Only two survived, Darth Bane, and a young girl Zannah whom he would take as his apprentice. After seeing how the bickering between his fellow Sith had led to their demise, Bane decreed that from that day forward there would be only two Sith at any one time: one Dark Lord and one apprentice. The Sith went into hiding, and the galaxy was at (relative) peace for nearly a millennium.

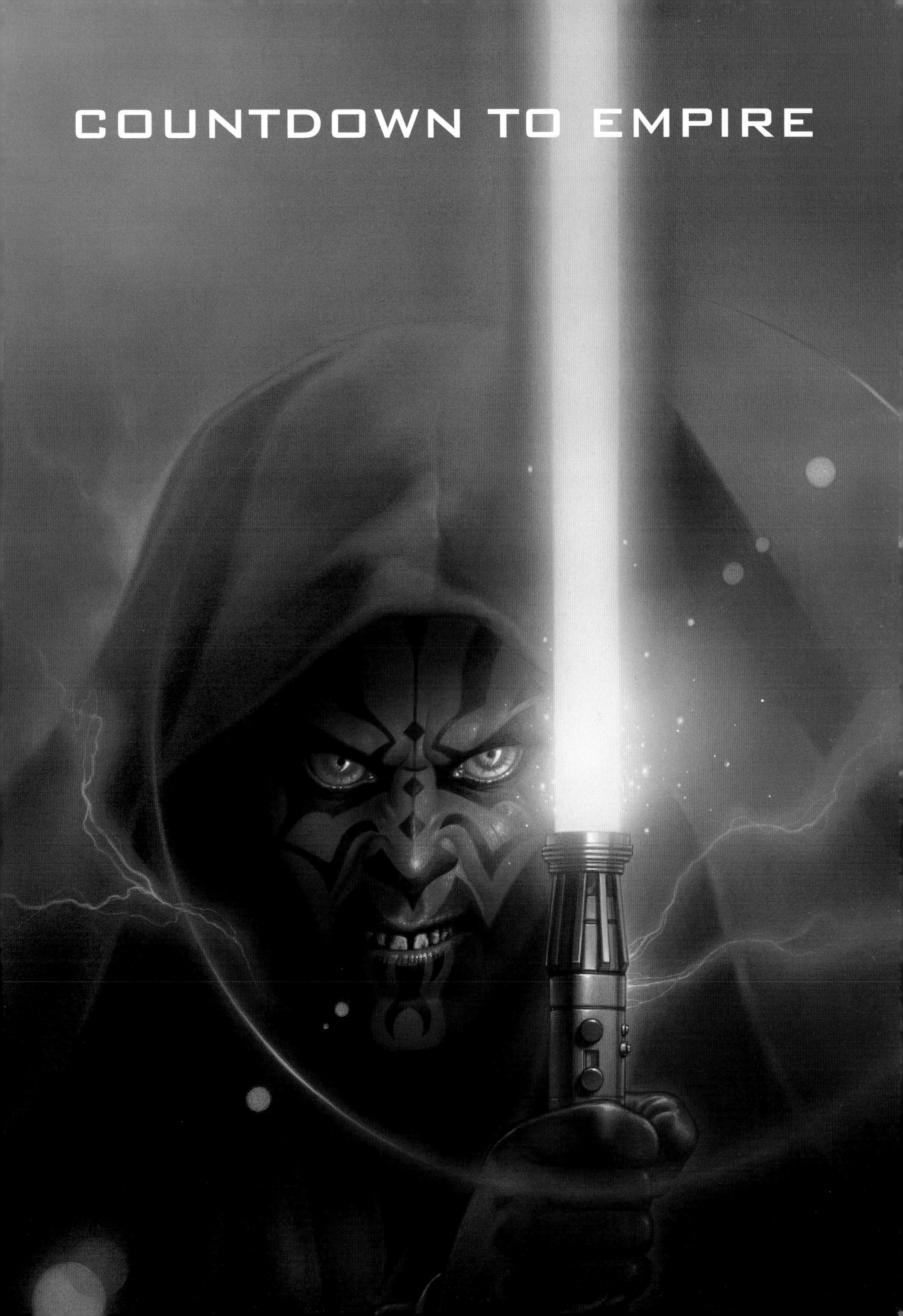
COUNTDOWN TO EMPIRE

NEW THREATS, NEW HEROES

Entering into the time period surrounding the Prequel Trilogy (Episodes I–III), Dark Horse (and indeed all of the *Star Wars* licensees) faced challenges in the form of limitations set by Lucasfilm. Obviously, it would not be in their interest to have events in the films "spoiled" in other media, so certain characters and events were deemed temporarily untouchable. The trick for us was to find ways to turn the limitations into advantages.

Previous page: art by Tsuneo Sanda. Star Wars Tales *Volume 5 (2005).*

Fortunately, Lucasfilm had anticipated the needs of its licensees, and each was given a minor film character with which to play. Jedi Council member Ki-Adi-Mundi was Dark Horse's go-to hero leading up to the release of *The Phantom Menace*.

Another character provided by Lucasfilm was former Jedi Padawan turned Jedi-hating bounty hunter Aurra Sing. If you blinked, you might have missed her appearance during the Podracer sequence in *The Phantom Menace*, but Sing went on to star as the villain in a number of stories, having a rich, full life in the EU.

Script by Tim Truman, pencils by Davidé Fabbri, inks by Christian Dalla Vecchia, colored by Dave McCaig, lettering by Steve Dutro. Star Wars #29 (2001), *and collected in* The Hunt for Aurra Sing (2002).

Her specialty was killing Jedi—and taking their lightsabers as trophies.

She even crossed lightsabers with Ki-Adi-Mundi on one or two occasions.

The knowledge that the Sith had returned after nearly a thousand years was a concern for the Jedi.

But even before they became aware of the existence of Darth Maul and his unseen Master, members of the Jedi Council were already unknowingly confronting the plots and machinations of Darth Sidious.

Script by Randy Stradley, pencils by Davidé Fabbri, inks by Christian Dalla Vecchia, colored by Dave McCaig, lettering by Steve Dutro. Jedi Council: Acts of War #1 *(2000) and the collection of the same name (2001). Following: art by Jon Foster.* Star Wars #39 *(2002) and* The Stark Hyperspace War *(2002).*

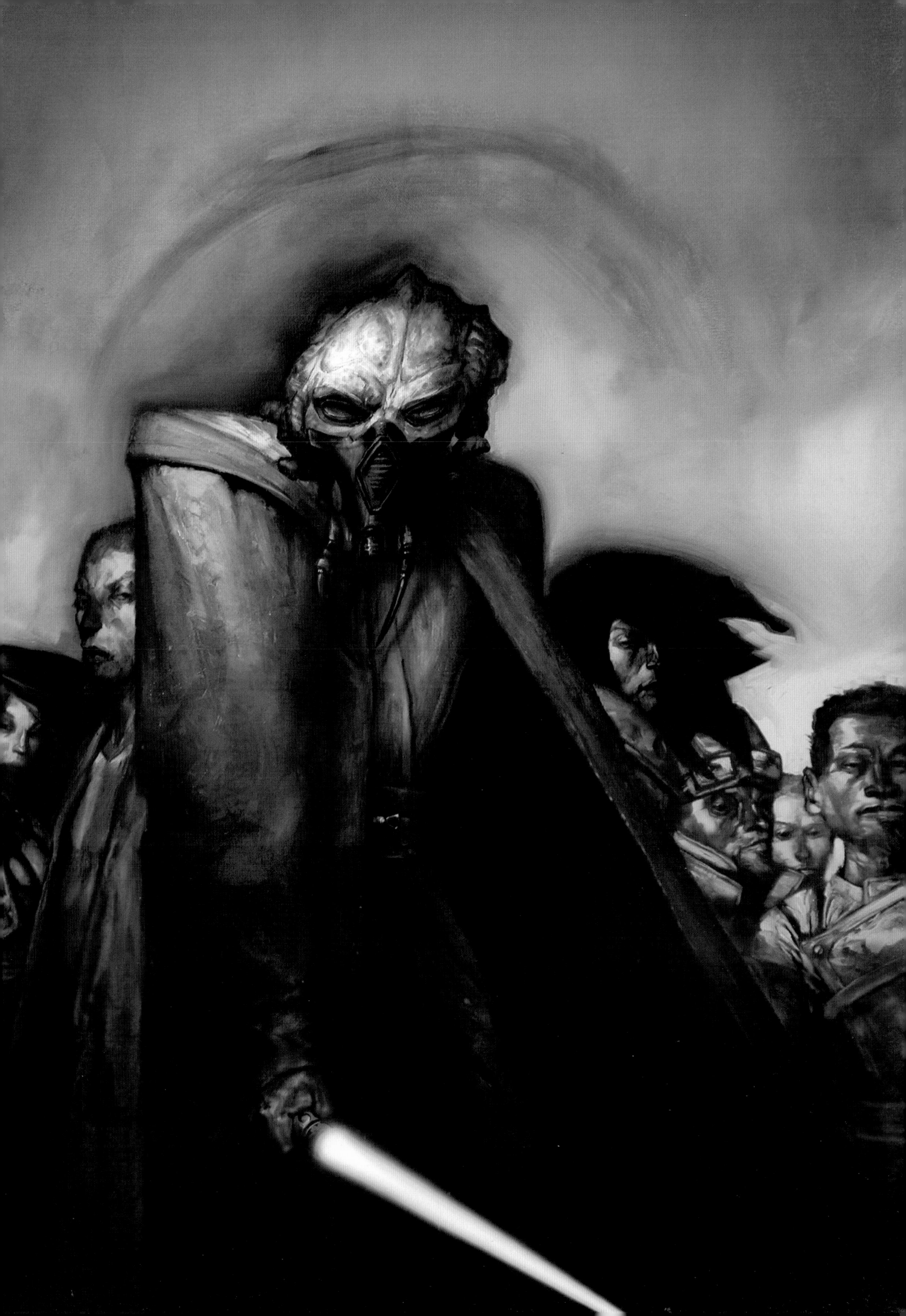

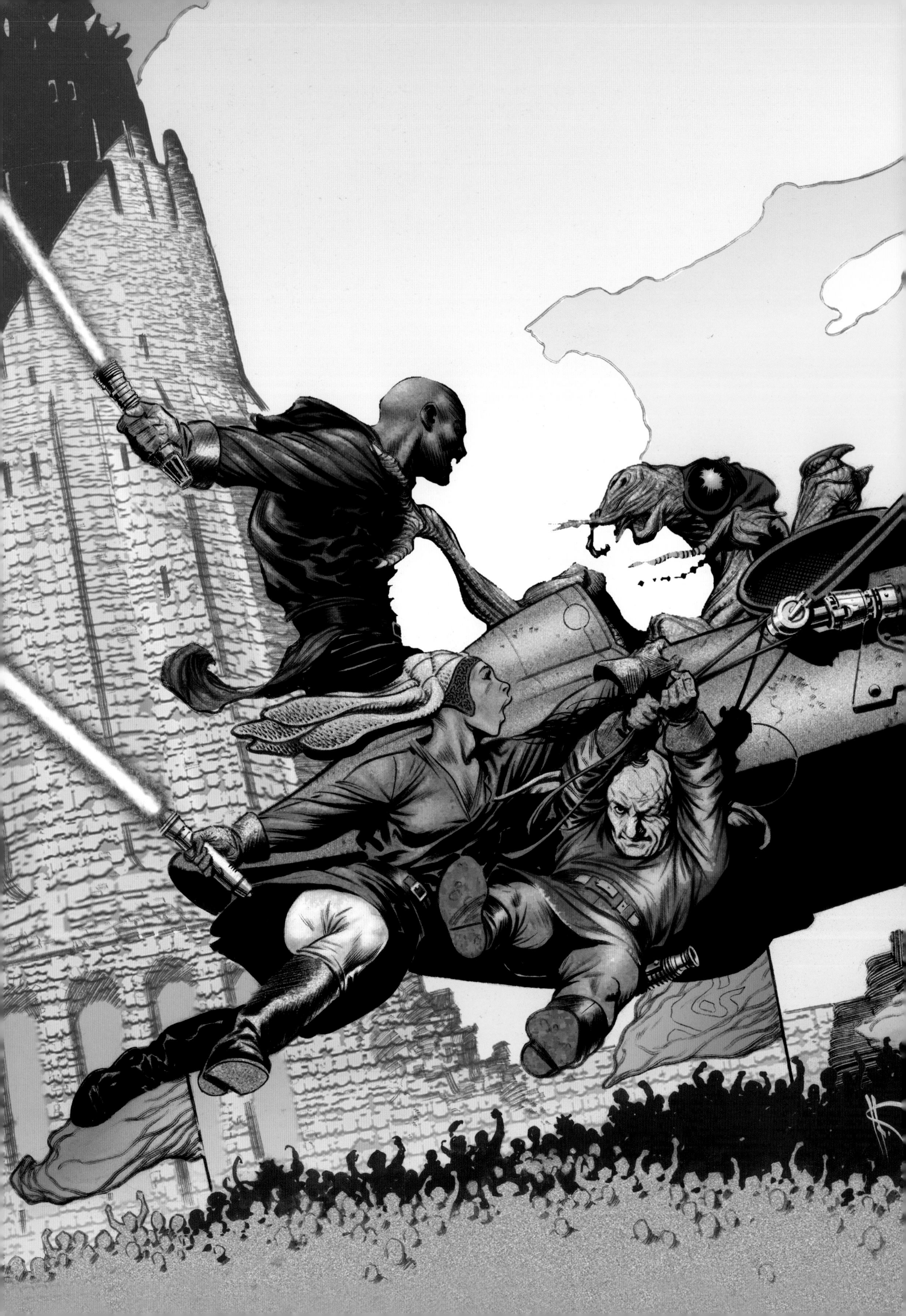

Expanding upon the lives of film characters was only a small part of what Dark Horse added to the *Star Wars* canon. New characters like self-exiled Jedi and Tusken Raider leader Sharrad Hett and his son A'Sharrad Hett were introduced. Note: taking on a krayt dragon armed only with a gaderffi (the traditional Tusken bantha-herding stick) is not recommended for novices.

Previous page: art by Mark Schultz. Star Wars *#15 (2000). This page: script by Tim Truman, pencils by Rod Pereia, inks by Stephen Hawthorne, colored by Dave McCaig, lettering by Steve Dutro.* Star Wars *#10 (1999), collected in* Outlander *(2001).*

The supporting cast grew rapidly. Whiphid Padawan K'Kruhk learned a trick or two from then-Jedi Council member Micah Giiett (whose untimely death opened a seat on the council for Ki-Adi-Mundi) . . .

Script by Randy Stradley, pencils by Davidé Fabbri, inks by Christian Dalla Vecchia, colored by Dave McCaig, lettering by Steve Dutro. Jedi Council: Acts of War #1 *(2000) and the collection of the same name (2002).*

MASTER
K'KRUHK.

MASTER
WINDU.
GREETINGS.

WE HAD
THOUGHT YOU
SLAIN WITH YOUR
TROOPS ON
TEYR.

I'M GLAD TO
HEAR YOU LIVE --
BUT SADDENED THAT
YOU NO LONGER
WALK WITH US.

WHY?

. . . as well as from Council leader Mace Windu. Shortly after the beginning of the Clone Wars, K'Kruhk had a crisis of conscience and abandoned the fight—until Mace convinced him to return to the fold. Considering how things ultimately turned out for the Jedi, K'Kruhk may have been better off keeping his own counsel.

Script by John Ostrander, pencils by Jan Duursema, inks by Dan Parsons, colored by Brad Anderson, lettering by Digital Chameleon. Jedi: Mace Windu *(2003)* and Clone Wars *Volume 1 (2003).*

THE CLONE WARS

No event in *Star Wars* history has been more anticipated than the Clone Wars. When it was revealed after the release of Episode II: *Attack of the Clones* (in which the Clone Wars began) that Episode III would jump ahead three years to the *end* of the war, the writers, artists, and editors at Dark Horse saw an opportunity to play in a time period relatively unfettered by existing continuity. Sure, some of the major players had restrictions placed on them, but the Clone Wars involved the whole galaxy, and there were lots of participants whom readers had not met—because we hadn't created them yet!

K'Kruhk wasn't the only Jedi to make a decision he or she would later regret. During one battle, A'Sharrad Hett learned Anakin Skywalker's guilty secret about slaughtering the Tuskens on Tatooine (*Attack of the Clones*). Hett hoped that by offering understanding and a sympathetic ear, he could convince Anakin to do the right thing and confess his crime to the Jedi Council . . .

Art by Jan Duursema and Brad Anderson. Republic #59 (2003), and appears in Clone Wars *Volume 3 (2004).*

51

... but Hett's revelation of his true human identity beneath his Tusken mask wasn't enough to sway Skywalker. Hett could have blown the whistle on him, but he believed Anakin would, in time, relieve himself of his own burden of guilt. Coulda, woulda, shoulda. Hindsight's always twenty-twenty.

 Script by John Ostrander, pencils by Jan Duursema, inked by Dan Parsons, colored by Brad Anderson, lettering by Sno Cone Studios. Republic #59 (2003), Clone Wars Volume 3 (2004).

Other major players made their first (and sometimes only) appearances in the pages of comic books. Among them, Master Tholme, the defacto head of the Jedi intelligence network. He was responsible for sending undercover Jedi into dangerous situations to learn of the Separatists' plans. But he was not above putting himself in the line of fire when necessary—and he had the scars to prove it.

Zao was a blind Jedi who made a point of going where the Force took him, regardless of what was happening in the galaxy around him. The Veknoid Master supported himself selling his soup—the flavor of which often revealed more about the taster than its ingredients.

Script by John Ostrander, pencils by Jan Duursema, inked by Dan Parsons, colored by Brad Anderson, lettering by Michael David Thomas. Republic #72 (2005) and Clone Wars *Volume 8 (2006).*

Sora Bulq was a Jedi who joined Count Dooku's Separatists—and the dark side. Here he fights Council member and top Jedi strategist Oppo Rancisis. Bulq killed the snake-bodied Thisspiasian Jedi, but later got what was coming to him.

Art by Jan Duursema, colored by Brad Anderson. Republic #75 (2005).

55

What would the Clone Wars be without clones?

Script by John Ostrander, pencils by Jan Duursema, inked by Dan Parsons, colored by Brad Anderson, lettering by Michael David Thomas. Jedi: Shaak Ti *(2003) and* Clone Wars *Volume 2 (2003).*

But not all clones were created equal. ARC Troopers (Advance Recon Clones) were proof of that. The ARCs were a small company of clones bred to be less docile than the average clone, and were personally trained by Jango Fett. What they lacked in numbers they made up for in tenacity . . .

This page and the following: script by Haden Blackman, pencils by Stephen Thompson, inked by Ray Kryssing, colored by Brad Anderson, lettering by Digital Chameleon. Republic #50 (2003) *and* Clone Wars *Volume 1 (2003).*

. . . and attitude. Anakin Skywalker eventually nicknamed this particular ARC Trooper "Alpha," and convinced the clone to give names to the clone officers he would go on to train . . .

... explaining why, later in the war, this Clone Commander is known as "Cody" instead of "2224." (Commander Cody, one of the unsung heroes of the Battle of Sarrish, later tried to kill Obi-Wan Kenobi on Utapau, per Palpatine's infamous Order 66.)

This page: script by Randy Stradley, art by Douglas Wheatley, colored by Ronda Pattison, lettering by Michael David Thomas. Following page: art by Sean McNally. Both from Free Comic Book Day 2006: Star Wars *(2006).*

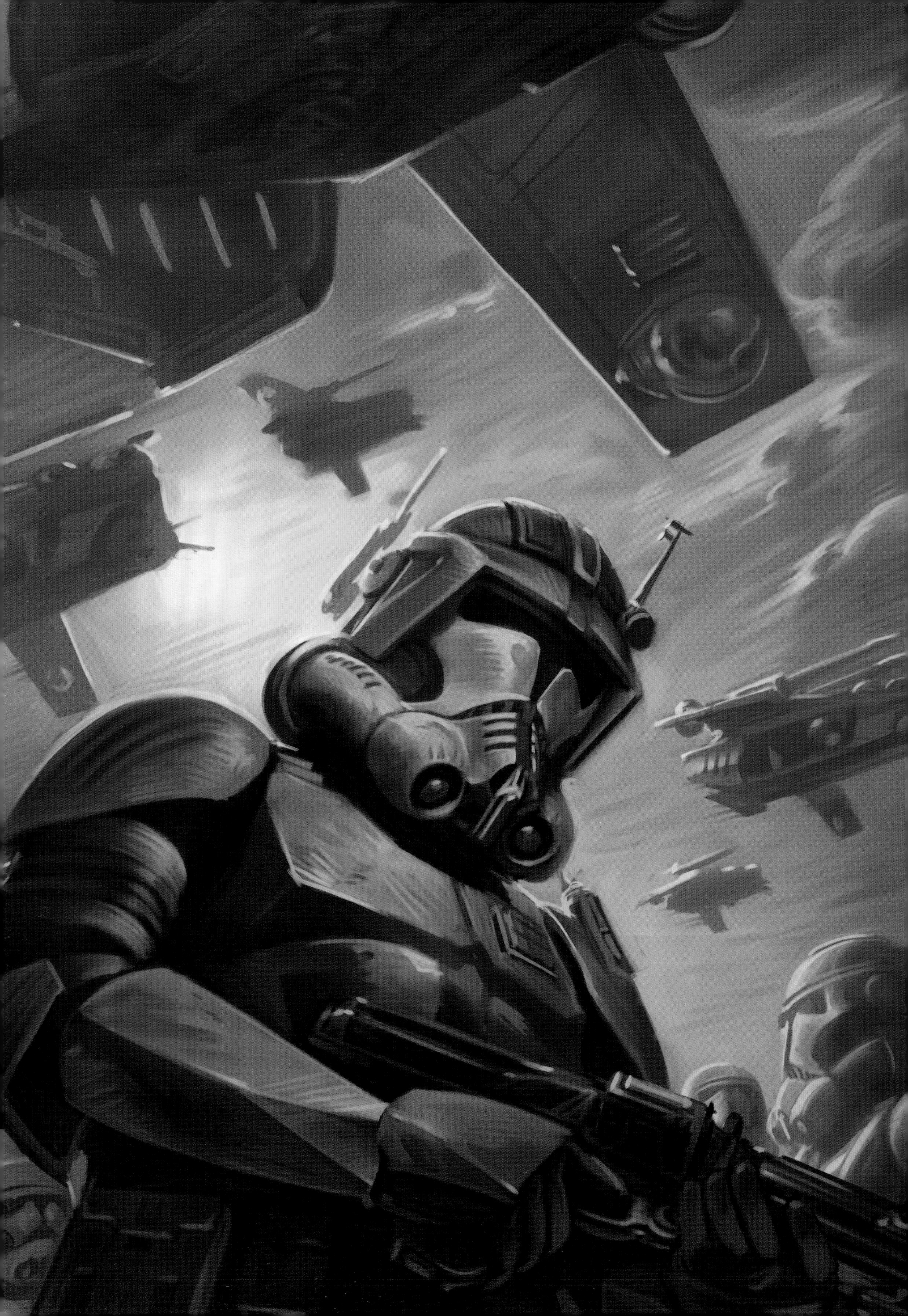

In *Jango Fett: Open Seasons*, writer Haden Blackman skillfully wove many of the disparate (and now impossible) elements of what had previously been Boba Fett's origin story and made them Jango's. The result not only repaired a rip in *Star Wars* continuity, but turned the elder Fett into an anti-hero fans could feel good about rooting for. Above, his family murdered by renegades, young Jango has his first encounter with Mandalorians.

Script by Haden Blackman, pencils by Ramon Bachs, inked by Raul Fernandez, colored by Brad Anderson, lettering by Digital Chameleon. Jango Fett: Open Seasons #1 and the collected volume of the same title (2002).

As the war progressed, the ranks of the bad guys swelled, as well. Asajj Ventress had already raised an army and conquered a planet when Count Dooku took her under his wing. She wanted desperately to become a Sith, but was never initiated into the secrets of that dark religion.

Ventress had a special hatred for the Jedi, and time and again Dooku unleashed her raw fury on the Republic's defenders. She went toe-to-toe with Anakin Skywalker several times, and it was she who gave him the lightsaber scars he bore in *Revenge of the Sith.*

Script by John Ostrander, pencils by Jan Duursema, inked by Dan Parsons, colored by Brad Anderson, lettering by Michael David Thomas. Republic #71 (2004) *and* Clone Wars *Volume 6 (2005).*

But always Ventress's main target was Obi-Wan. She despised him more than any other adversary . . . because he understood her, and pitied her.

Art by Jan Duursema, colored by Brad Anderson. Republic #70 (2004).

Another of Dooku's pawns was the seemingly unkillable bounty hunter Durge.

Art by Brian Ching, colored by Brad Anderson. Obsession #2 (2004).

Anakin faired better against Durge than most. Ouch.

 Script by Haden Blackman, art by Brian Ching, colored by Sno Cone Studios, lettered by David Michael Thomas. Obsession #3 (2004) and Clone Wars *Volume 7* (2005).

In fact, there's little question that without the efforts of Obi-Wan and Anakin, the Republic would have had a much tougher time fighting the war. Either singly, or in tandem, they eventually accounted for Darth Maul, Asajj Ventress, Durge, Count Dooku, and . . .

. . . General Grievous.

Art by Brian Ching, colored by Brad Anderson. Obsession #4 (2005).

They were an unbeatable team—until Anakin went all dark side. But let's not get ahead of our story. Before we leave the Clone Wars, there are two more characters who deserve special notice . . .

SAME PATH, DIFFERENT ENDS

From 2000 to 2005, across the pages of more than sixty individual comic books, Aayla Secura and Quinlan Vos were the mainstays of Dark Horse's line. Aayla was the pure one, always striving to do right. Quin had a dark side, one that burned to confont and destroy evil, but which also led him to be seduced by its power. Born out of a need for characters who could carry on in the comics while Anakin and Obi-Wan were busy in films, prose novels, and other media, the two Jedi came to exemplify the struggle between order and expediency that would eventually (with a little help from the Sith) bring down the Republic. Along the way, the two characters attracted the attention of George Lucas himself, which led to roles for each of them in the movies . . . almost.

Opposite page: Art by Jan Duursema and Dave McCaig. Star Wars #44 *(2002) and* Rite of Passage *(2003).*

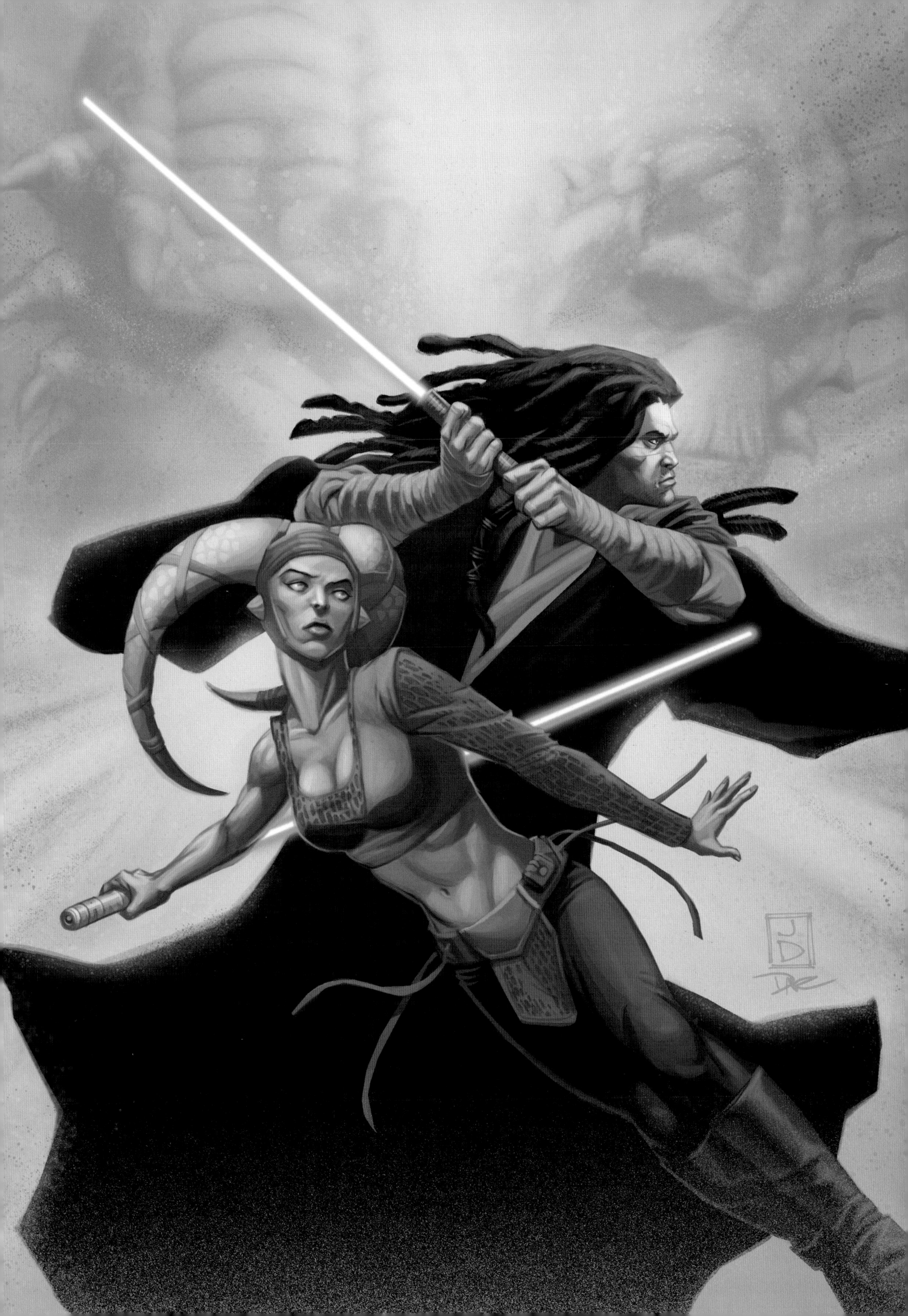

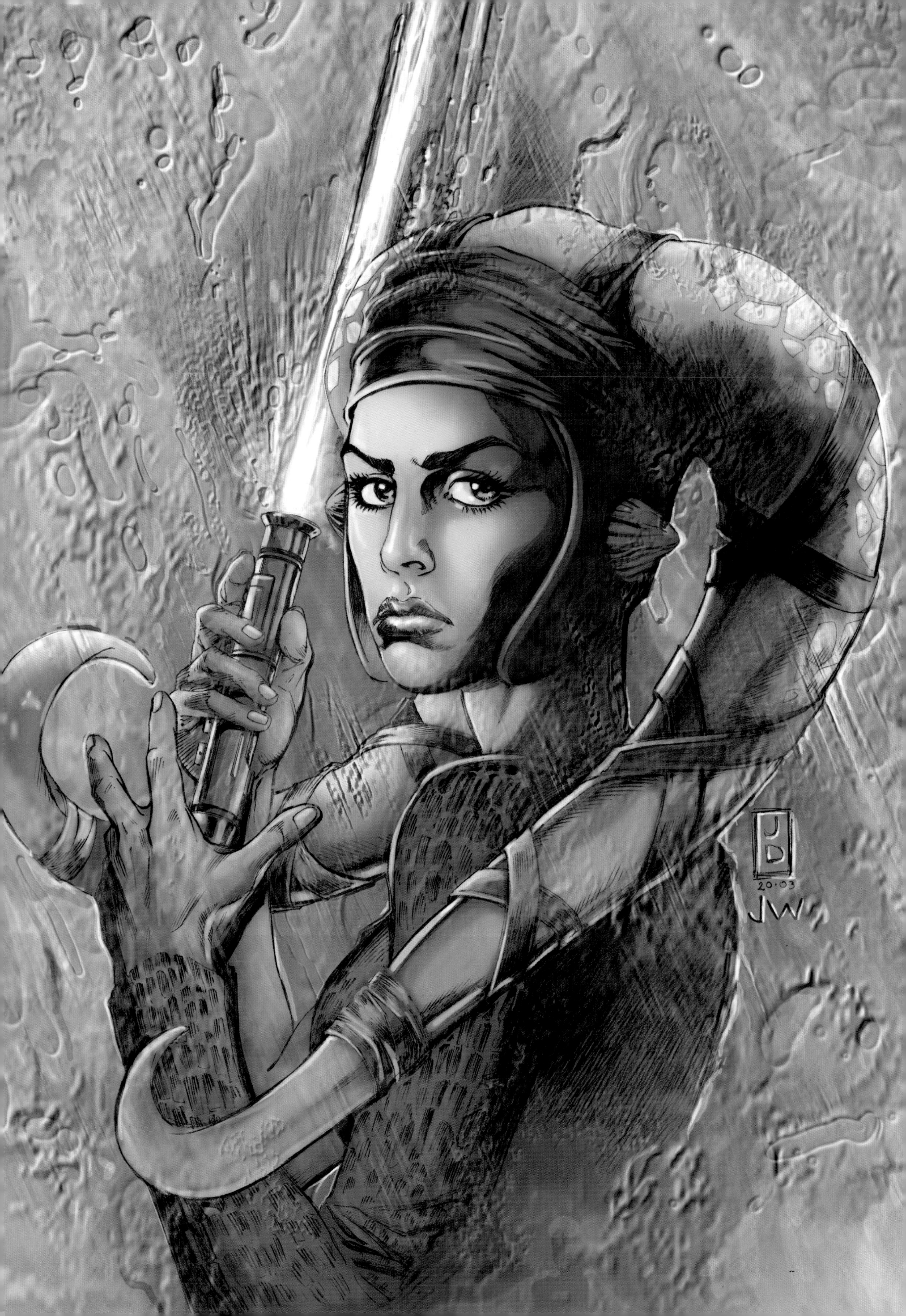
JD
20·03
JW

Having taken a shine to Aayla after her early appearances in the comics, Lucas gave her a cameo part (where she was played by actress Amy Allen) in the Arena Battle in *Attack of the Clones*. When artist and Aayla's co-creator Jan Duursema drew the comics adaptation of the film, she put Quinlan Vos in the scene, too.

Opposite: art by Jan Duursema, colored by Brad Anderson. Jedi: Aayla Secura *(2003) and* Clone Wars *Volume 4 (2004). This page: script by Henry Gilroy, pencils by Jan Duursema, inked by Ray Kryssing, lettering by Steve Dutro.* Attack of the Clones *(2002).*

In a way, Vos actually appeared on screen before Aayla. In the film *The Phantom Menace*, in the marketplace scene on Tatooine, there is a swarthy, dangerous-looking character sitting with the Podracer pilot Sebulba. Duursema liked the way he looked, and used him as a template for Vos. The character's appearance has since been canonized in the Expanded Universe as Vos being on an undercover assignment and not being able to acknowledge Qui-Gon Jinn's presence.

Quinlan Vos was Jedi spymaster Tholme's Padawan when he first made Aayla's acquaintance. Though just a child, she instinctively reached out to Vos through the Force when a wampa attacked. After that adventure, Tholme brought her into the Jedi order, thus rescuing Aayla from a life of servitude.

Script by John Ostrander, pencils by Jan Duursema, inked by Ray Kryssing, colored by Brad Anderson, lettering by Digital Chameleon. Star Wars #42 (2002) and Rite of Passage *(2003).*

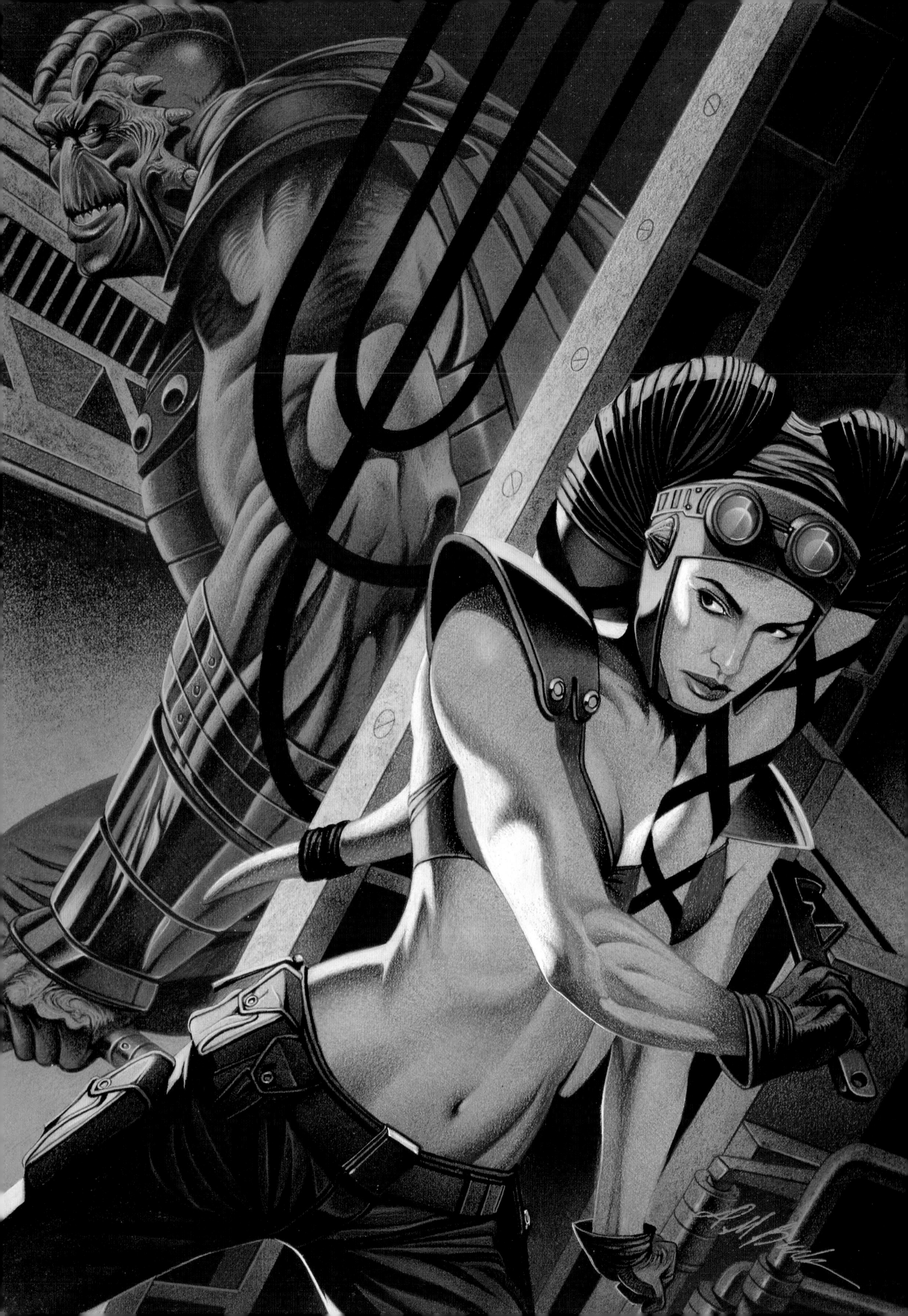

Aayla and Quin took on many different intelligence assignments. Sometimes they infiltrated the strongholds of the enemy alone, and sometimes they used others—with or without that person's willing cooperation—to carry out the mission. One of Vos's favorite operatives was Vilmarh "Villie" Grahrk, a Devaronian rogue whose services were available to the highest bidder—or the most threatening employer. In fact, though the Jedi did not know it, Villie had once worked for Darth Sidious.

Opposite page: art by David Michael Beck, colored by Brad Anderson. Republic #72 (2004) *and* Clone Wars *Volume 8 (2006). This page: script by John Ostrander, pencils by Jan Duursema, inked by Ray Kryssing, colored by Dave McCaig, lettering by Steve Dutro.* Star Wars #32 (2001) *and* Darkness *(2002).*

To recount all of the adventures that Aayla, Quin, and Villie had—together and singly—would require an entire book larger than this one. We can only hope to cover the highlights. For instance, the story in which they were first introduced had both Quin and Aayla struggling to recall who they were, after the Twi'lek villain Chom Frey Kaa wiped their memories with the drug glitteryll. Before Aayla fully recovered, she fell under the thrall of the Anzati Dark Jedi, Karkko.

This page: art by Andrew Robinson. Twilight *(2001). Opposite: art by Jon Foster.* Star Wars *#35 (2001) and* Darkness *(2002).*

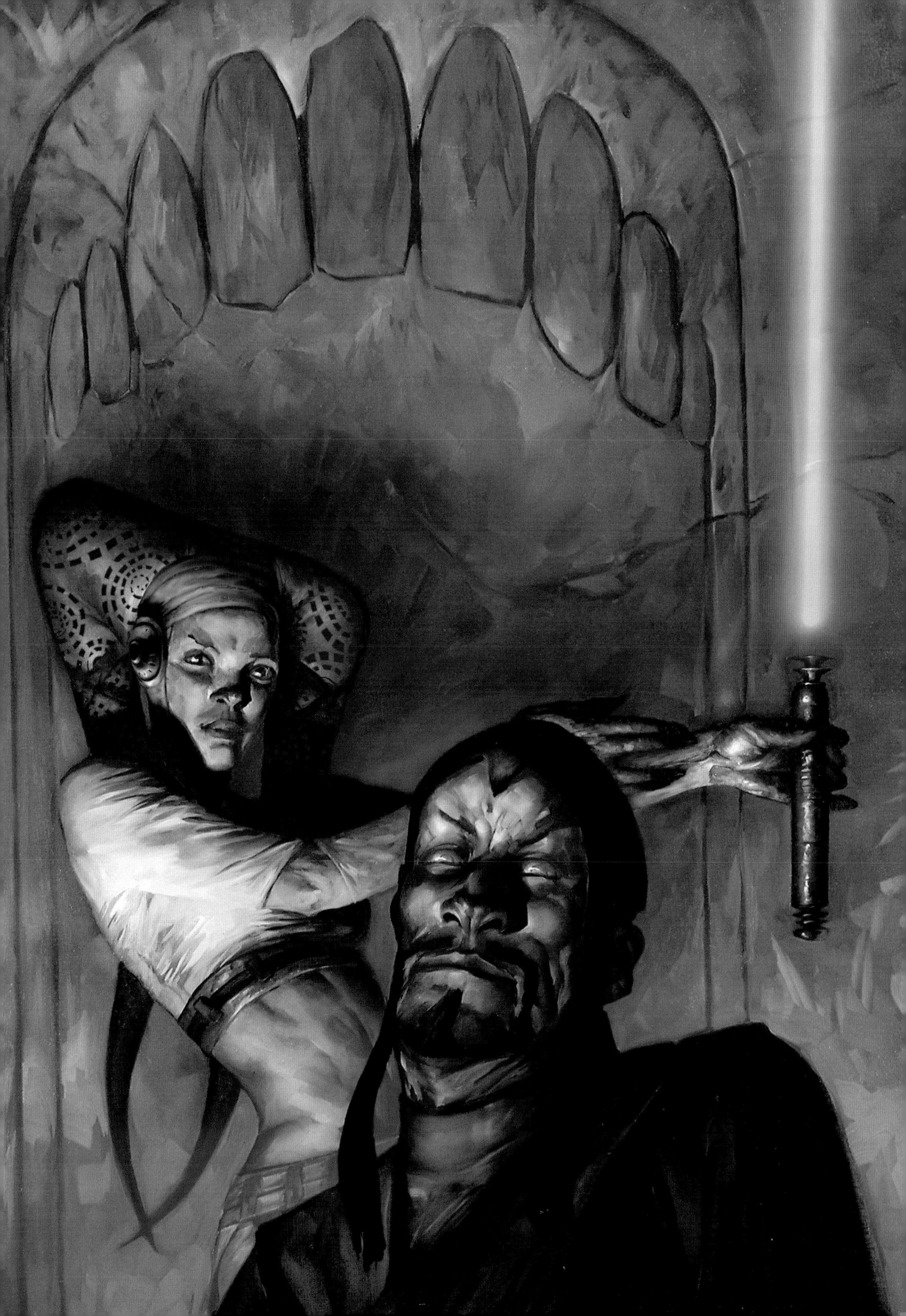

By the beginning of the Clone Wars, Aayla had regained her memories—and her free will—even against the mind-controlling pheromones of a Falleen adversary.

Script by John Ostrander, art by Jan Duursema, colored by Brad Anderson, lettering by Digital Chameleon. Republic #49 (2003), *collected in* Clone Wars *Volume 1 (2003).*

But as time went by, Quin's undercover infiltration of Count Dooku's inner circle led him to the dark side . . .

THAT SMELL... OZONE? LIGHTSABER!

THE WHIPID KNOWS. TOO LATE. BEFORE THE SITH WAKES UP, BEFORE HE CAN STOP ME, BEFORE ANYONE CAN STOP ME --

-- I WILL KILL THE SITH!

NO!

THE SITH WAKES. THE MOMENT IS PASSING. TOO SOON IT BECOMES TOO LATE!

. . . where his mania to uncover the identity of Dooku's Sith Master made Quinlan Vos susceptible to Dooku's manipulation—even to the point that he assassinated a senator whom Darth Sidious and Dooku wanted removed. Master K'Kruhk tried to protect the senator, and was wounded for his troubles. (I wonder, is that hat just to keep K'Kruhk's head dry?)

Script by John Ostrander, pencils by Jan Duursema, inked by Dan Parsons, colored by Brad Anderson, lettering by Michael David Thomas. Republic #63 (2004) and Clone Wars *Volume 4 (2004).*

Eventually, though, with the help of Aayla, Tholme, Obi-Wan Kenobi, the entire Jedi Council, and the love of a good woman (Khaleen Hintz, pictured), Quin was able to reach the same point of clarity Aayla had come to . . . twenty-seven issues earlier.

Script by John Ostrander, pencils by Jan Duursema, inked by Dan Parsons, colored by Brad Anderson, lettering by Michael David Thomas. Republic #76 (2005), collected in Clone Wars *Volume 8 (2006).*

. . . just in time for he and Aayla to lead Republic troops to an important victory on Saleucami.

Art by Jan Duursema, colored by Brad Anderson. Republic #76 (2005), collected in Clone Wars *Volume 8 (2006).*

And then came Episode III. While the main story of the film concerned itself with events which would shape the galaxy for years to come, the backdrop of the ongoing Clone Wars provided an occasion for Obi-Wan to tell Anakin, "Saleucami has fallen, and Master Vos has moved his troops to Boz Pity."

Art by Tsuneo Sanda. Episode III: Revenge of the Sith *(2005).*

An early draft of the screenplay for *Revenge of the Sith* had Aayla leading troops on Felucia, and Quin going to Kashyyyk along with Master Barriss Offee to help defend the Wookiee homeworld.

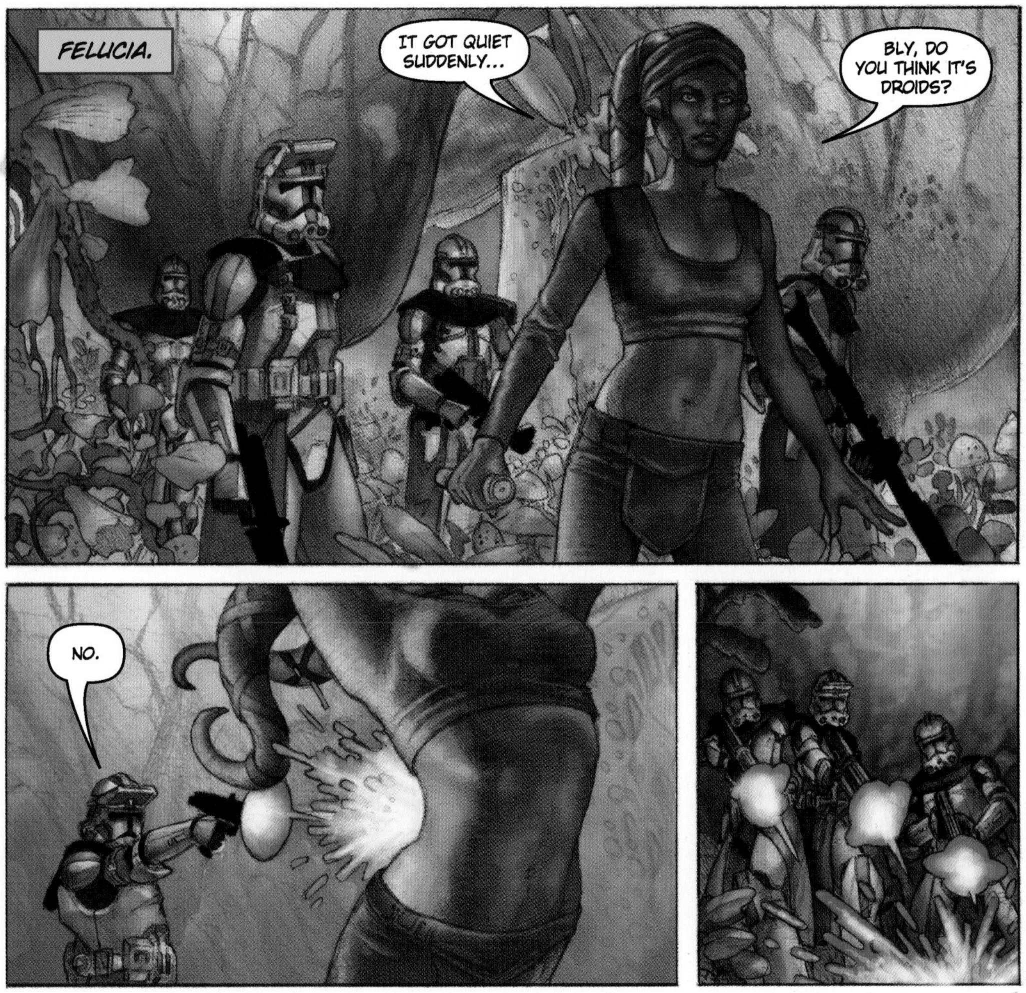
FELUCIA.
IT GOT QUIET SUDDENLY...
BLY, DO YOU THINK IT'S DROIDS?
NO.

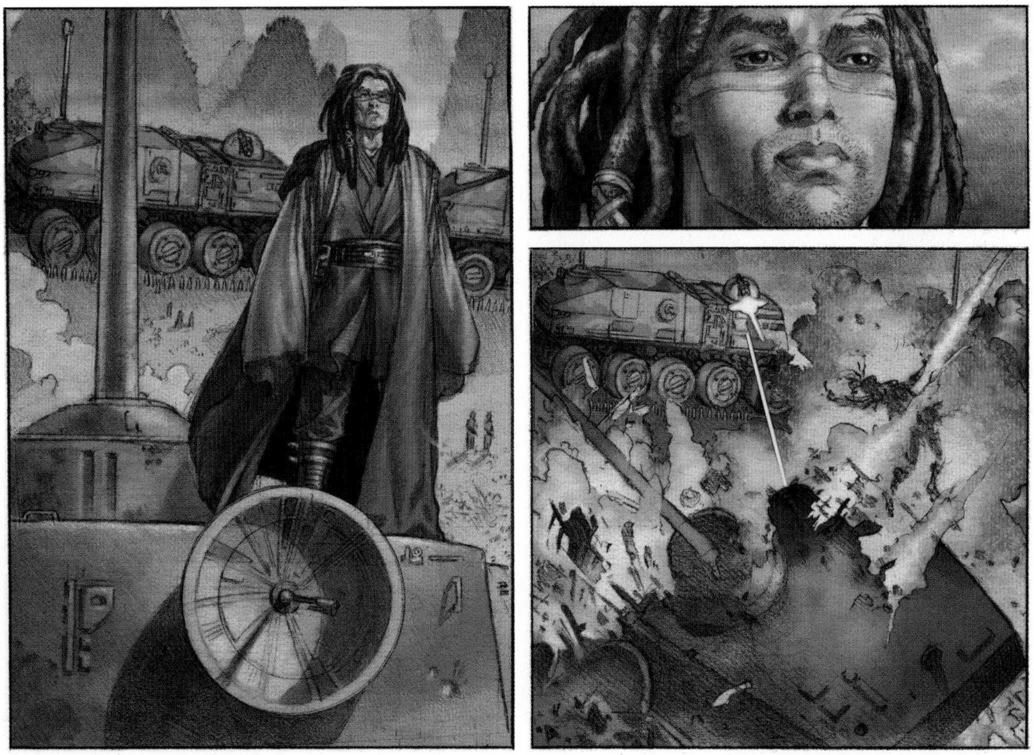

The draft also had both Jedi dying at the hands of their troops after Palpatine gives Order 66 to his clone commanders. It wasn't until just before publication of the comics adaptation of the film that we at Dark Horse learned that the decision had been made to cut Quin's scene from the final shooting script. So, in the pages of the *Revenge of the Sith* comics and graphic novel, Quinlan Vos meets his end . . .

Script by Miles Lane, art by Douglas Wheatley, colored by Chris Chuckry, lettering by Michael David Thomas. Revenge of the Sith *(2005).*

. . . or not. We received word that it was permissible for Quinlan Vos to survive Order 66. So, a new "end" was created for the character. Quin survived the attack by his own troops and, grievously wounded, escaped the clone troopers who were hunting him and . . . well, Villie tells it better . . .

Will Quin, Khaleen, little Korto, "Uncle" Villie, and Masters Tholme and T'ra Saa live happily ever after? Only time will tell.

Script by John Ostrander, pencils by Jan Duursema, inked by Dan Parsons, colored by Brad Anderson, lettering by Michael David Thomas. Republic #83 (2006) and Clone Wars *Volume 9 (2006).*

The same goes for the handful of other surviving Jedi. Palpatine's "Jedi purge" was phenomenally successful. According to official estimates, approximately 97% of the Jedi were gunned down by their own troops. The rest took it on the lam. Except for Master Zao (in panel 3, above) who, unnoticed, continued to follow the "living Force."

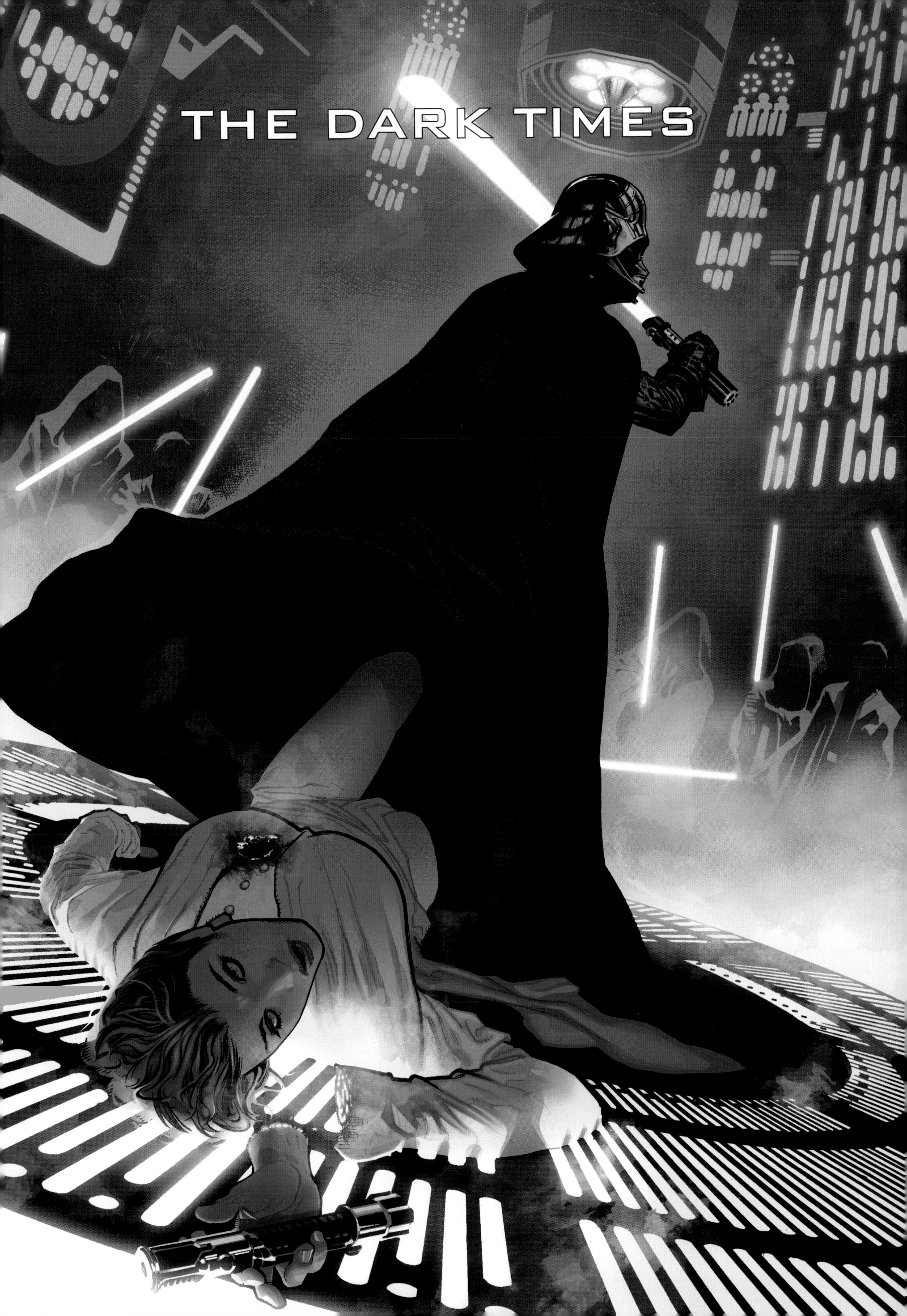
THE DARK TIMES

UNKNOWN REGIONS

Though not officially recognized as a separate era on the *Star Wars* timeline (see page 191), the nineteen years between the time Anakin Skywalker becomes Darth Vader and the time Luke Skywalker first picks up his father's lightsaber have long been off-limits to *Star Wars* licensees, with only minor excursions being allowed. Now that *Revenge of the Sith* has been released, limited portions of this time period have been opened for exploration—a situation that has both fans and creators excited. As of this writing, Dark Horse has begun what we hope will be a long journey into this great unknown.

Previous page: art by Adam Hughes. Purge *(2005) and* Clone Wars *Volume 9 (2006).*

Of course, it's not all unknown. Its beginning and its end are well-established now, as are some of its major players.

From a plot by Welles Hartley, script by Mick Harrison, art by Douglas Wheatley, colored by Ronda Pattison, lettering by Michael David Thomas. Dark Times #1 (2006).

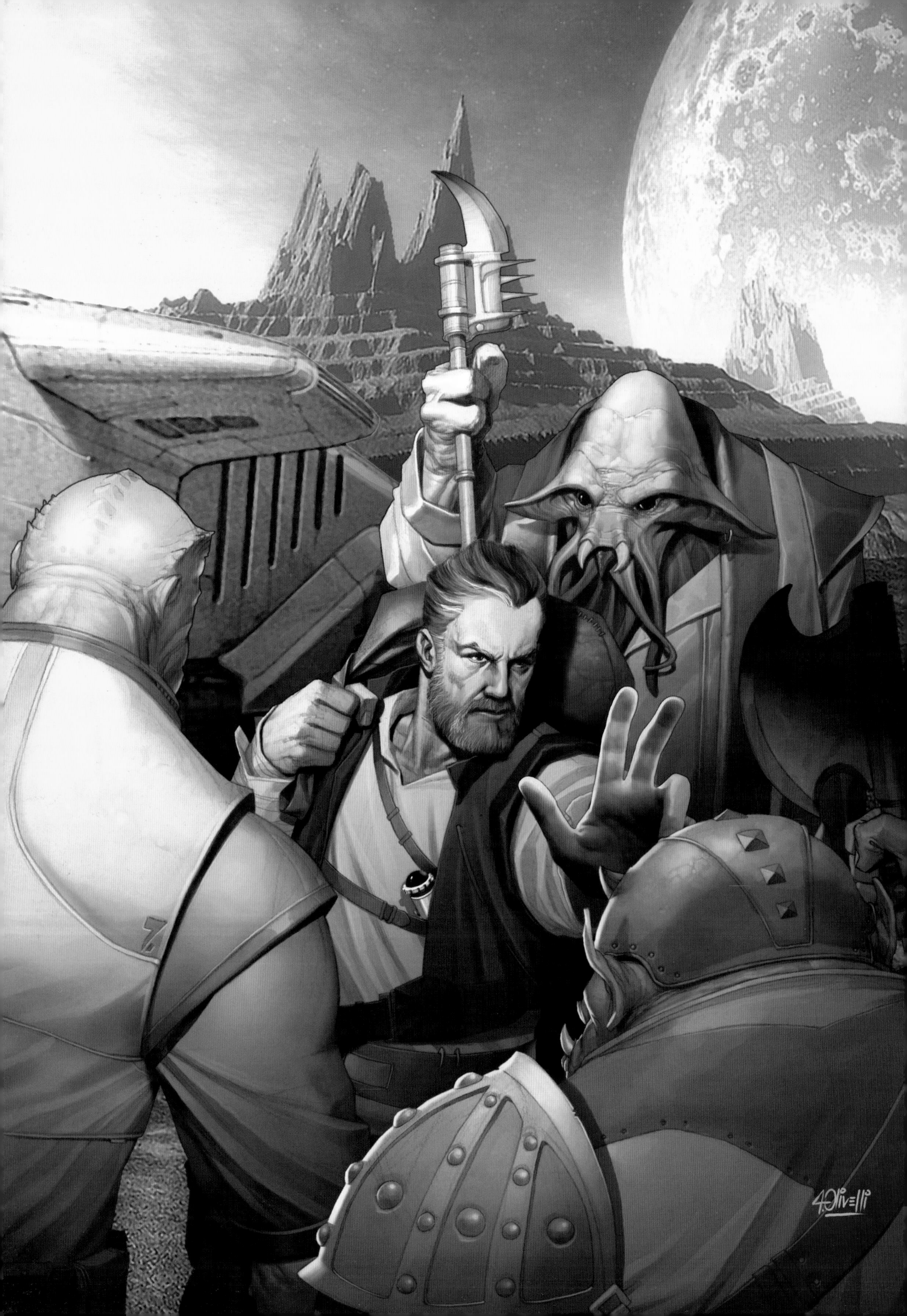

But, with Obi-Wan Kenobi confined to Tatooine and Yoda sequestered on Dagobah for the duration, most of the weight of the era falls on Vader's shoulders. But as powerful and iconic as he may be, we don't want to overburden him with stories that might become "routine" with repetition. Especially when . . .

Opposite: previously unseen art from a "Dark Times" proposal which was part of a presentation Dark Horse gave to Lucas Licensing executives in 2003. Art by Ariel Olivetti. This page: art by Douglas Wheatley. Dark Times #2 (2007).

. . . there are so many other characters whose stories can be told!

For our first foray into the "dark times," we chose Nosaurian Separatist-turned-freedom-fighter Bomo Greenbark and human ex-patriot, ex-General Jedi Knight Dass Jennir as our focus characters. Former enemies, the two became fast friends.

The two met when Jennir was on the run from the clone troops he had once led against Bomo and his friends. Obviously, it was Greenbark's kind understanding of Jennir's plight that formed a bond of trust between them.

This page: script by Welles Hartley, art by Douglas Wheatley, colored by Chris Chuckry, lettering by Michael David Thomas. Republic #79 (2005) *and* Clone Wars Volume 9 (2006). *Facing: art by Douglas Wheatley.* Dark Times #3 (2007).

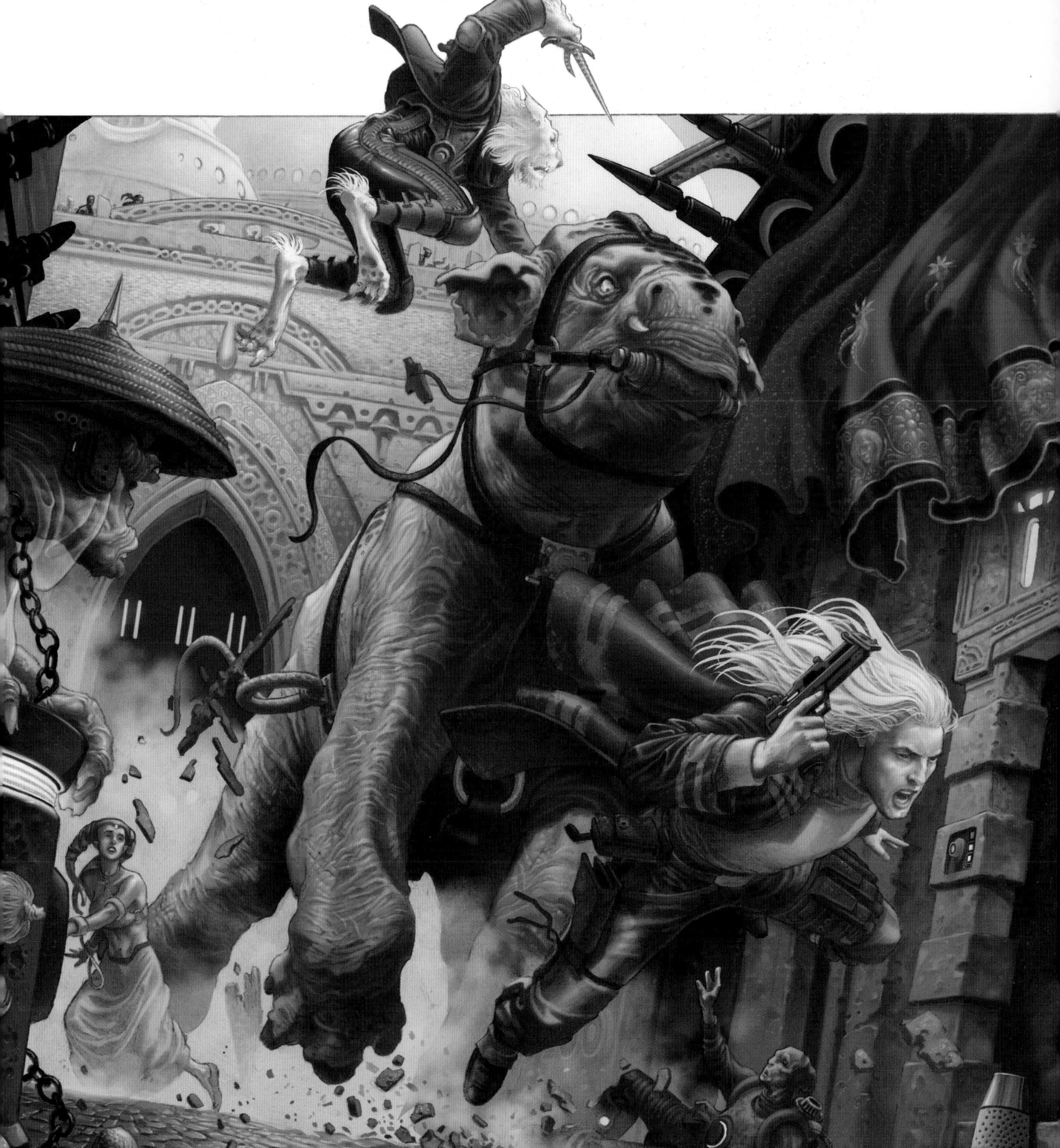

Whether that bond can be maintained is a question for the future. But whatever becomes of Greenbark and Jennir, it is certain that there are many other characters waiting for their moment on the stage. As of this writing, it is still early days in the *Dark Times* series.

This page: art by Douglas Wheatley. Dark Times #5 (2007). Opposite: plot by Welles Hartley, script by Mick Harrison, art by Douglas Wheatley, colored by Ronda Pattison, lettering by Michael David Thomas. Dark Times #1 (2006).

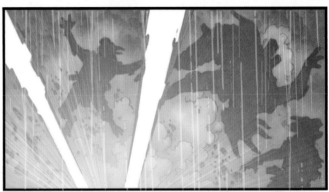

WE SURRENDER.

Our next three stops along the *Star Wars* timeline all involve characters established in the films. Approximately fourteen years after they were last seen in *Revenge of the Sith*, C-3PO and R2-D2 became involved in a series of adventures (well, okay, misadventures) that spanned the next five years. The explanation for the droids' absence from Captain Antilles' watchful eye was finally established on starwars.com's "What's the Story" fan competition.

Meanwhile, years before he put the "death mark" on Han Solo, Jabba the Hutt had already built his criminal empire—and a reputation for making deals that no one alive could turn down. The closest the Great Jabba came to not being one step ahead of his adversaries was when a competitor unleashed a swarm of intelligent, weasel-like Freckers on him.

Three years BBY ("Before the Battle of Yavin," you'll recall), Boba Fett had his first encounter with Darth Vader. It should be noted that Anakin Skywalker encountered young Boba Fett during the Clone Wars, so he knew who was under the Mandalorian helmet. Of course, Fett had no idea that Vader was actually Skywalker. And, though they squared off against each other at the time, it would not be long before Fett's self-interest had him side with Vader in another situation.

Art by Ken Kelly. Boba Fett: Enemy of the Empire *(1999) and the trade paperback of the same title (1999).*

Here's the portion of the book where we allow Boba Fett a few pages in which to strut his stuff.

Art by Tsuneo Sanda. Boba Fett: Man with a Mission *(2007).*

Besides being *Star Wars*'s most beloved anti-hero, Boba Fett is second only to Vader as a favorite subject of artists.

This page: art by Cam Kennedy. Boba Fett: Bounty on Bar-Cooda *(1995), collected in* Boba Fett: Death, Lies, and Treachery *(1998). Opposite: art by Adam Hughes.* Boba Fett: Overkill *(2006), collected in* Boba Fett: Man with a Mission *(2007).*

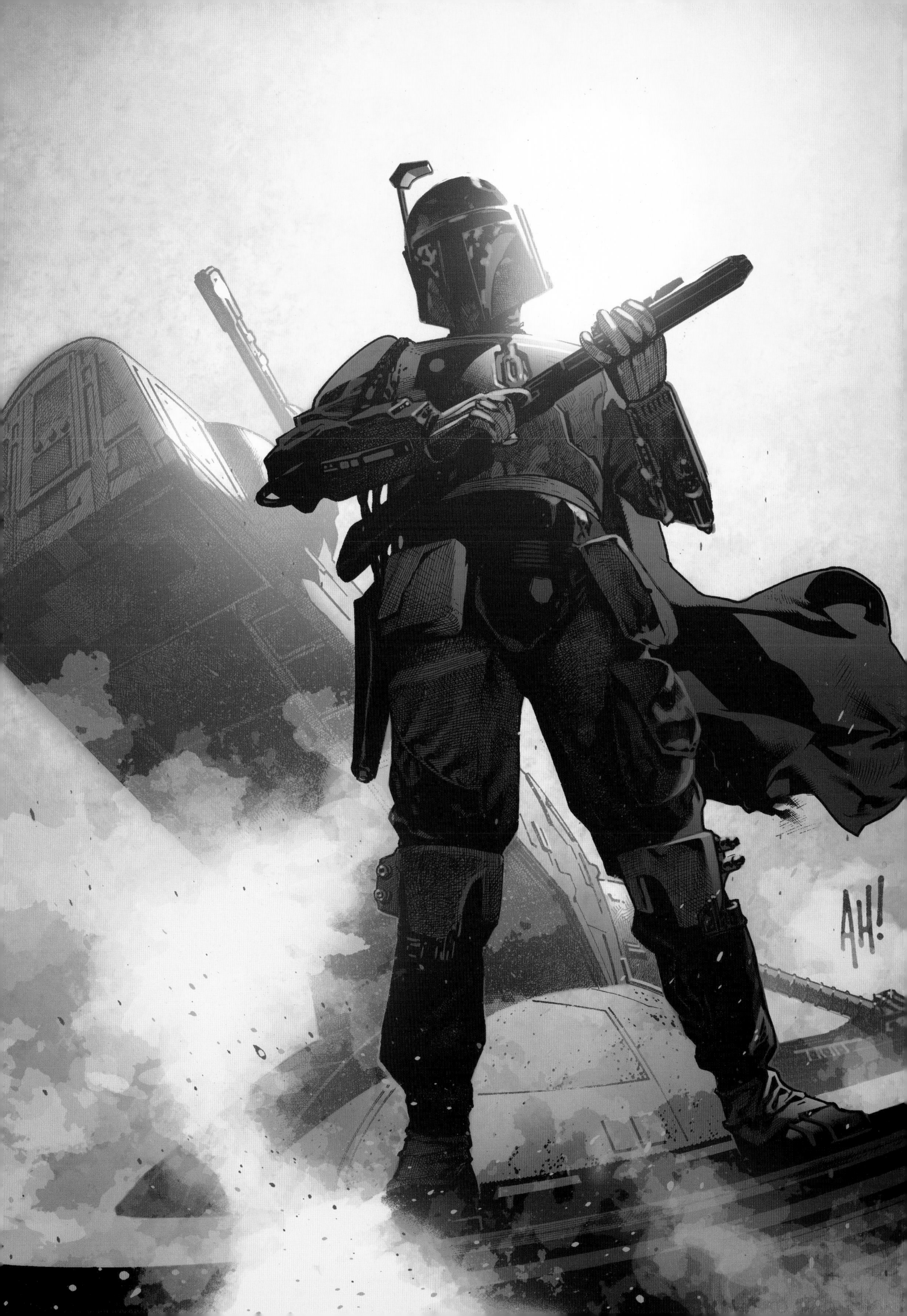
AH!

Some of them even got to paint him twice!

As proof you can't keep a good bad man down, Boba Fett escaped his *Return of the Jedi* movie death in the Sarlacc pit (twice, by some accounts), and went on to bedevil Han Solo and his friends for years to come. He has even become a mainstay in the *Legacy of the Force* novel series published by Del Rey.

But, before all that—one year BBY, to be exact—Boba Fett was charged with protecting Han Solo, Chewbacca, Lando Calrissian, and Greedo during a race to find the fabled Yavin Vassilika. Another example of Jabba the Hutt's self-interest at work.

True to his importance to the overall *Star Wars* mythos, Vader played another lead role at the far end of the nineteen-year period, as well.

Just a few weeks before the events in *A New Hope* took place, a cabal of disgruntled Moffs and Imperial officers plotted to assassinate both Palpatine and Vader. The lesson: never underestimate the Sith.

 This page: script by Scott Allie, pencils by Ryan Benjamin, inked by Curtis Arnold, colored by Dave Stewart, lettering by Michelle Madsen. Empire #1 (2002), *collected in* Empire Volume 1 (2003). *Facing page: art by Brian Horton.* Empire #2 (2002).

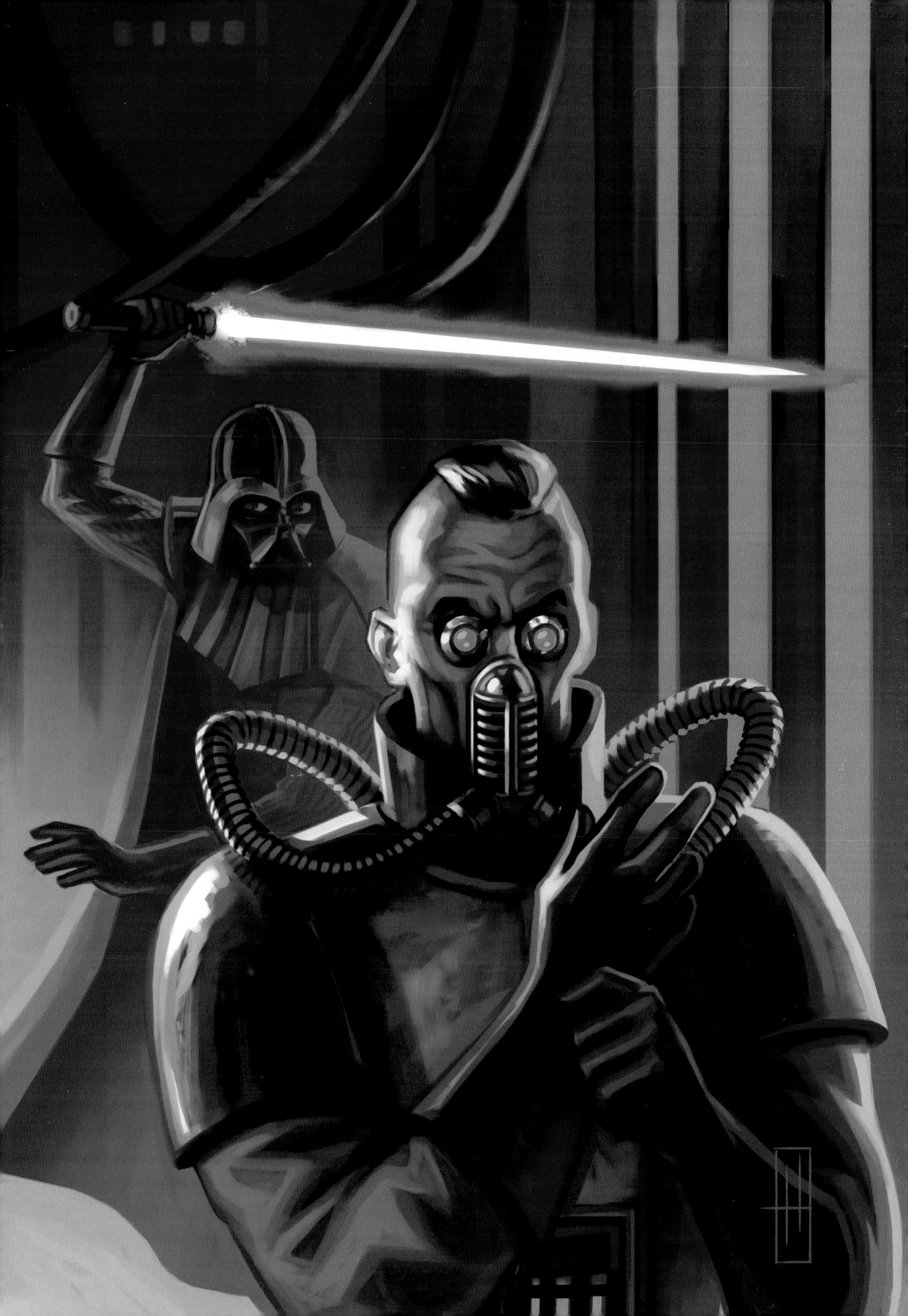

Not long after, in a story suggested by the events in the *Star Wars Radio Drama*, Princess Leia and her crew escaped Vader's clutches, only to find themselves in a standoff with other Imperials on the planet Kattada. The fellow with the tattooed "headband" is Basso, a Rebel agent who had the plans for the Death Star hypnotically encoded in his memory. The Rebellion had begun.

THE REBELLION

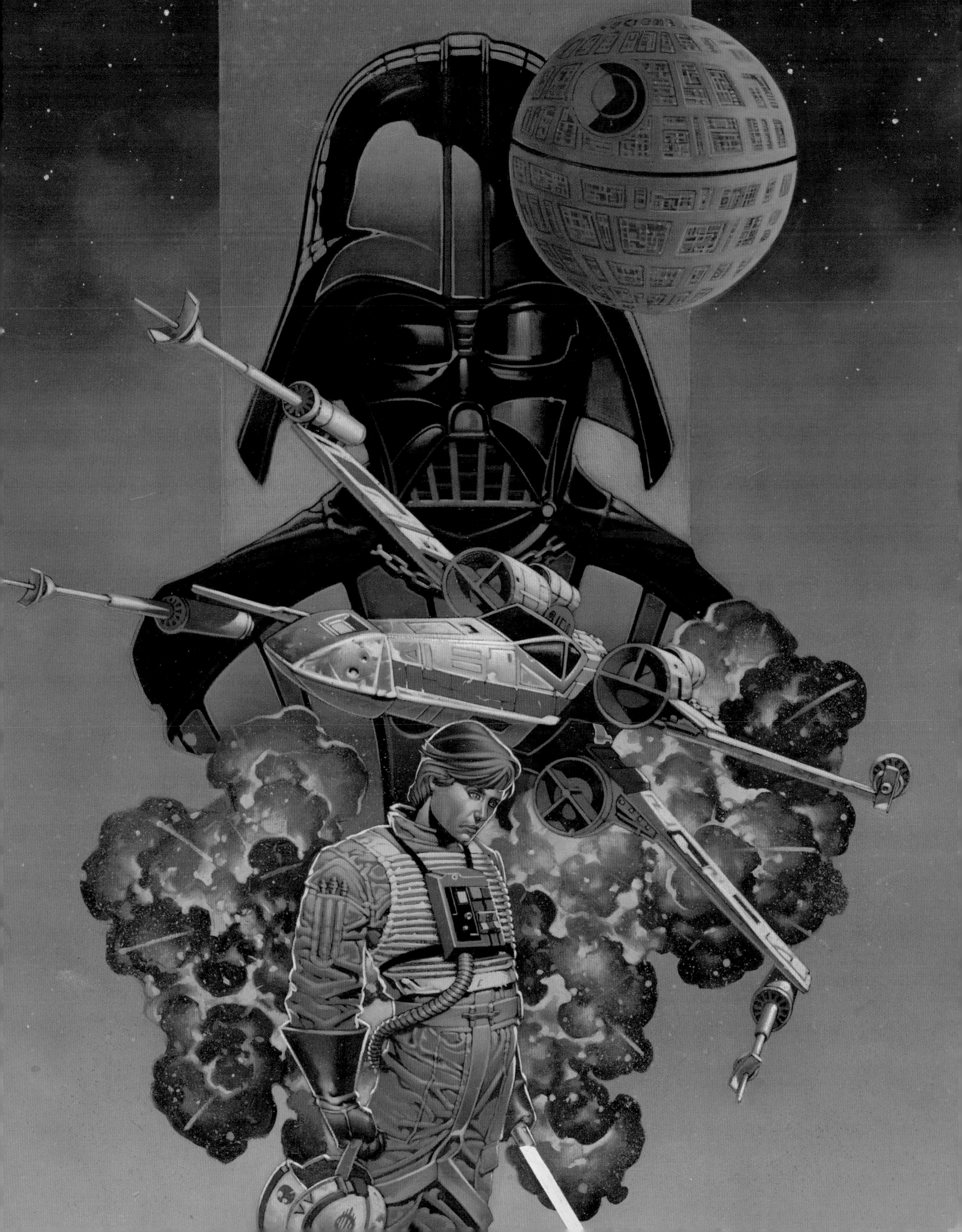

THE STAR WARS EVERYBODY KNOWS
. . . OR NOT

Though many (many!) stories have been told about the adventures of Luke Skywalker, Princess Leia, Han Solo, and the other stars of the original trilogy of *Star Wars* films, there are still substantial gaps in the timeline in which further tales can be told! When moving into these gaps, the tact we've tried to take is to establish new characters—who can someday play lead roles in their own stories.

Previous page: art by Tomás Giorello. Empire #34 (2005) *and* Empire Volume 6 (2006).

Which is not to say the "Big Three" (or Four, or Five, etc.) are any less important than they once were.

Art by Dave Dorman. Empire's End #1 and the collection of the same name.

117

Luke is still the lightning rod for adventure . . .

. . . Leia is still the heart and soul of the Rebellion . . .

Art by David Michael Beck, colored by Brad Anderson. Empire #21 (2004) and Empire Volume 4 (2005).

119

. . . Han Solo is still the coolest pilot in the galaxy. (Though, we tend to have a fairly flexible definition of "cool" here at Dark Horse.)

 This page: art by Tsuneo Sanda. Star Wars Tales *Volume 3 (2003). Facing page: art by David Michael Beck, colored by Brad Anderson.* Empire *#22 (2004), included in* Empire *Volume 4 (2005).*

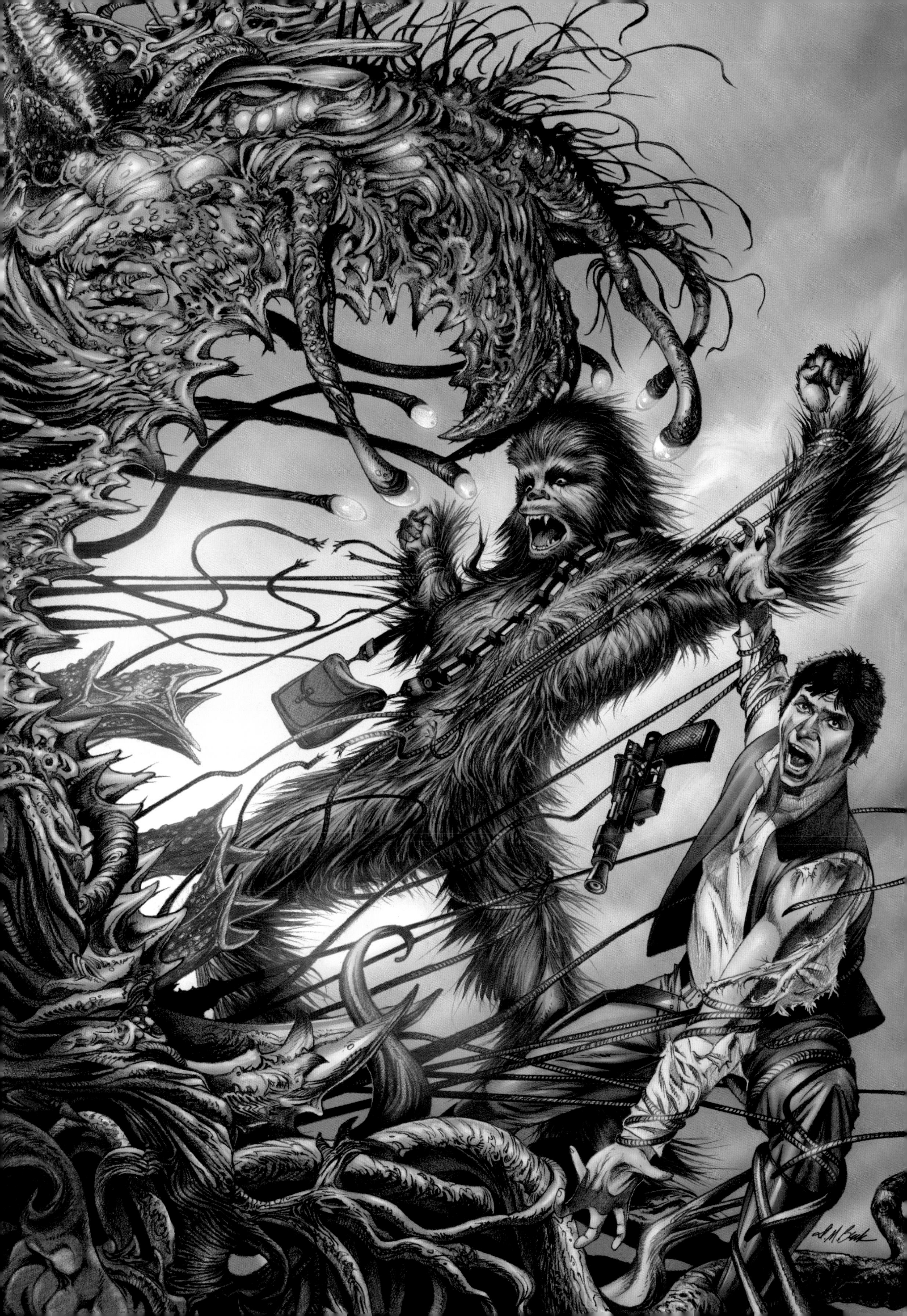

But whether alone or in a group, the heroes of the original films are but a part of a larger tapestry woven from story threads stretching across the galaxy.

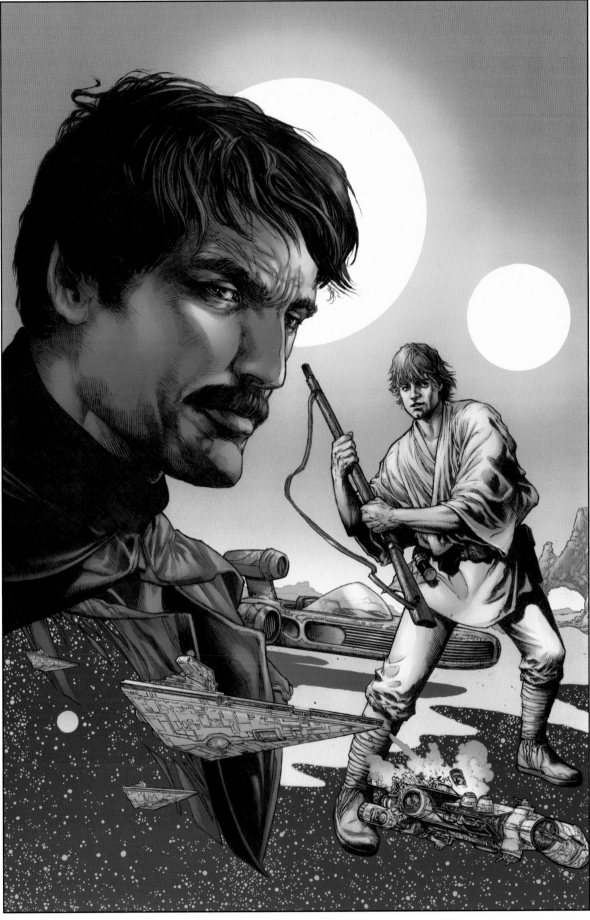

Though his part in *A New Hope* was largely cut in the final edit, Biggs Darklighter still fulfilled the pivotal role of Luke's wingman during the attack on the Death Star. In 2003, Dark Horse restored Biggs to his original place in the story, confirmed his boyhood history with Luke, and reconciled some long-unnoticed errors in Darklighter's own timeline.

Art by Douglas Wheatley, colored by Chris Chuckry. Empire #8 (2003).

Biggs was already a hero to the Rebellion before the Battle of Yavin. Among his exploits: the liberation of impounded X-wing fighters which were later used to attack the Death Star.

Both pages: script by Paul Chadwick, art by Douglas Wheatley, colored by Chris Chuckry , lettering by Sno Cone Studios. This page: Empire #12 (2003). *Opposite:* Empire #15 (2003). *Both collected in* Empire Volume 2 (2004).

BIGGS DARKLIGHTER HAS REVULSION LOADED ON HORROR, AS HE BREATHES IN THE PREDATOR'S *MOIST EXHALATIONS* AS ITS *JAWS CLOSE* IN *ON HIM.*

BLAST AFTER BLAST ENTERS THE CREATURE, UNTIL THE SMELL OF SEARED MEAT FILLS THEIR NOSTRILS ... BUT *STILL* IT FIGHTS.

BDOW BDOW BDOW

AAHHH!

DANTELS!

He and Red Squadron also helped acquire astromech droids for those X-wings. It was on that mission that he met smuggler Nera Dantels. Though the adventures they shared drew them to one another, Biggs' life ended before their relationship could blossom.

Later, Dantels and her ship *Starduster* played an important part in Luke and Leia's ill-fated mission to the planet Jabiim—a world where "Skywalker" was a dirty word, thanks to decisions Anakin has been forced to make during the Clone Wars.

Dantels' bravado and quick thinking make her a prime asset for the Rebellion. There is certainly more of her story to be told.

Script by Thomas Andrews, art by Adriana Melo, colored by Michael Atiyeh, lettering by Michael David Thomas. Empire #32 (2005), Empire *Volume 6 (2006).*

As the scope of the Rebellion widened, its ranks grew. But to recruit one soldier—a clone trooper who had been marooned on a jungle planet before Order 66 was given—Luke Skywalker was forced to impersonate a "Jedi General" circa the Clone Wars era.

The trooper, nicknamed Able, later joined Luke and the aforementioned Basso on a mission which required the whole team to disguise themselves as Imperial personnel.

Script by Welles Hartley, pencils by Davidé Fabbri, inks by Christian Dalla Vecchia, colored by Neziti Domenico, lettering by Michael David Thomas. Empire #38 (2005), Empire Volume 7 (2007).

It wasn't the first time—or the last—that Rebels donned Imperial mufti . . .

Art by David Michael Beck, colored by Brad Anderson. Empire #40 (2006).

For those of you keeping track: previous page, of course, Luke Skywalker. This page: General Roons Sewell, who preceded General Jan Dodonna as the Rebellion's chief strategist. Following pages: a Duros operative nicknamed "Mouse," and soon-to-be Red Squadron pilots Derek "Hobbie" Klivian and Biggs Darklighter . . .

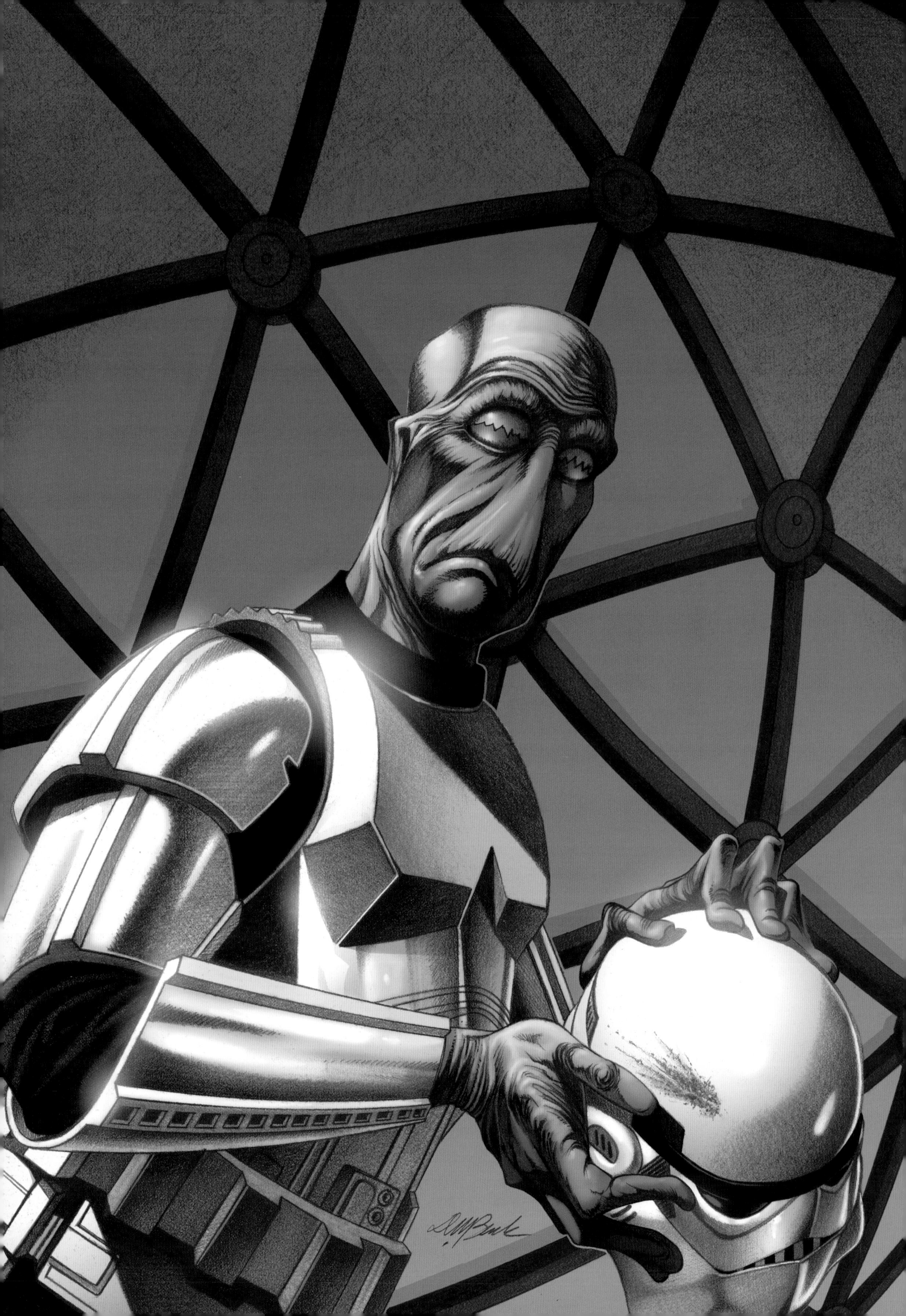

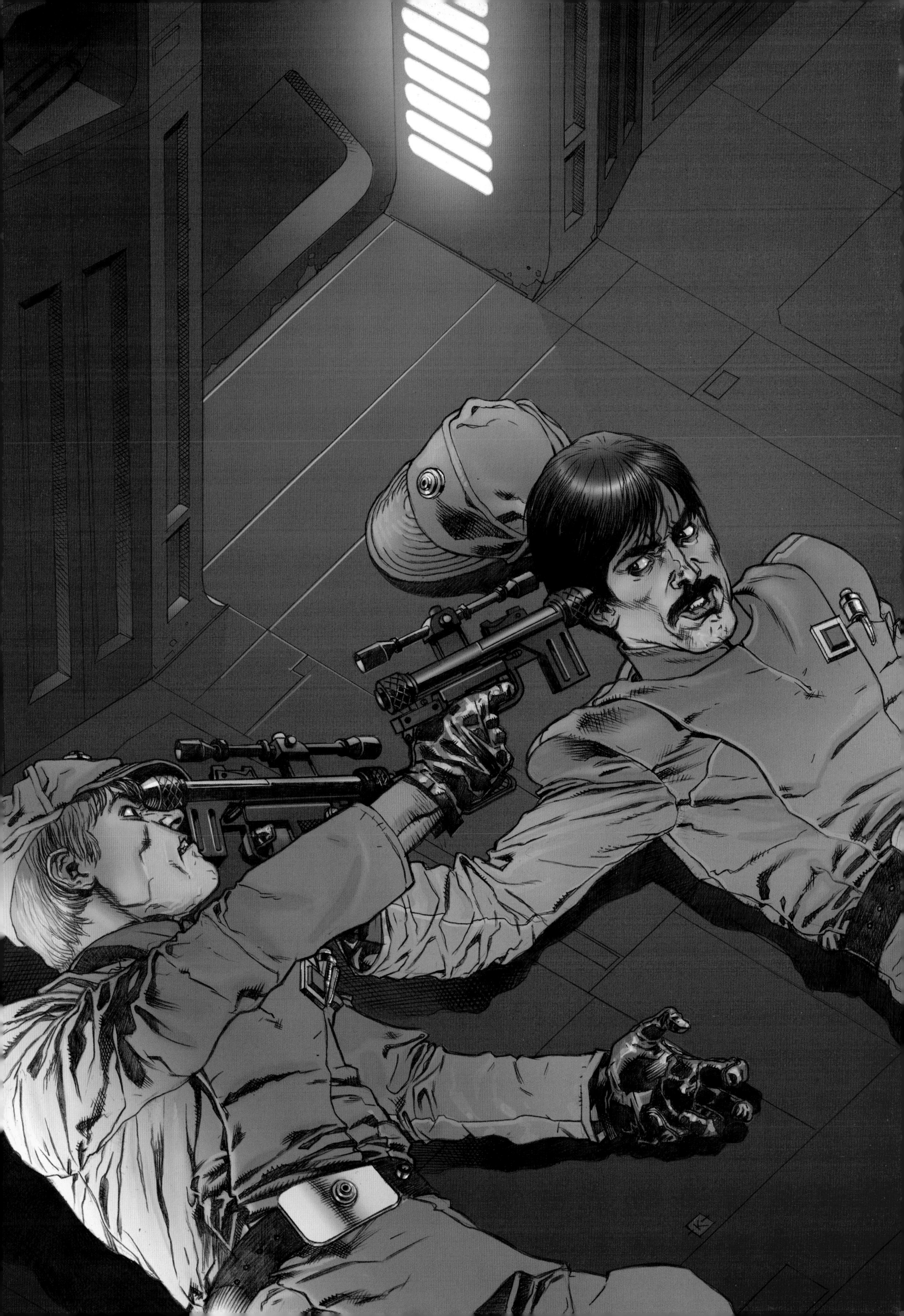

But not every mission required guile to defeat the enemy. Sometimes all it took was common, everyday courage and the belief in oneself. For instance, Deena Shan, whose career in the Rebellion began as a stock clerk, displayed the kind of pluck that soon led to bigger, more important—and more dangerous—missions.

Some more dangerous than she liked.

Art by Brandon Badeaux, colored by Wil Glass. Rebellion #3 (2006).

135

But the galaxy is a dangerous place, and there is no "safe middle" to be found—as spacer BoShek discovered. (You may remember him from the cantina scene in *A New Hope*.)

As in the Clone Wars, there were heroes on both sides—though some, like Imperial Lieutenant Janek Sunber, had their loyalties tested more than others.

Part of the fun of playing in the Expanded Universe is being able to surprise our readers with unexpected connections and revelations. With Janek Sunber, we established him as a man of common origins with an uncommon sense of right and duty. He became a bad guy the fans could root for.

Script by Welles Hartley, pencils and colors by Davidé Fabbri, inks by Christian Dalla Vecchia, lettering by Michael David Thomas. Empire #16 (2004) and Empire *Volume 3 (2004).*

Then, two years later we revealed that Sunber was Luke Skywalker's boyhood friend "Tank," (mentioned in passing in *A New Hope*). Luke ran into him during an undercover mission. But even after all of the deceptions were over, Luke was unable to convince Sunber to leave the Empire and join the Rebellion.

Script by Welles Hartley, pencils and colors by Davidé Fabbri, inks by Christian Dalla Vecchia, lettering by Michael David Thomas. Empire *#39 (2004) and* Empire *Volume 7 (2007).*

It was a failure that would come back to haunt Luke.

Art by Brandon Badeaux, colored by Wil Glass. Rebellion #1 (2006).

But there were plenty of other challenges to keep Luke—and the rest of the movie heroes—busy. *Shadows of the Empire* was billed as a "movie without the movie," and was remarkable especially for its behind-the-scenes logistics.

Art by Hugh Fleming. Shadows of the Empire #1 (1996) and the collection of the same name (1997).

Set in the period between *The Empire Strikes Back* and *Return of the Jedi*, it was a simultaneous telling of different parts of a larger story across three mediums: a novel, a video game, and comics. There were even toys, trading cards, and a soundtrack.

In addition to featuring favorite characters from the films, the story also introduced characters like Dash Rendar, Big Gizz and his swoop gang, and Prince Xizor, the dreaded head of the criminal organization Black Sun.

Art by Hugh Fleming. Shadows of the Empire #6 (1996) and the collection (1997).

The end of *Return of the Jedi* may have marked the end of Darth Vader, but the Empire was not about to go quietly.

Just days after the Battle of Endor, the pilots of Rogue Squadron were joined by Luke Skywalker for a reconnaissance mission to the Corellian system—that led to a battle with Imperials seeking revenge for the death of the Emperor.

Art by Gary Erskine. X-Wing: Rogue Leader #3 (2005) *and* Omnibus: X-Wing Rogue Squadron *Volume 1 (2006).*

After that, it seemed the Rogues, with Wedge Antilles in command, were in almost constant action. Whether in the skies above alien worlds . . .

Art by Dave Dorman. X-Wing: Rogue Squadron #2 (1995).

. . . on the ground, battling for every inch of gain . . . or in space, taking on the fleets of the Empire, they were never far from the frontlines fighting for the New Republic.

Art by John Nadeau. X-Wing: Rogue Squadron #24 (1997).

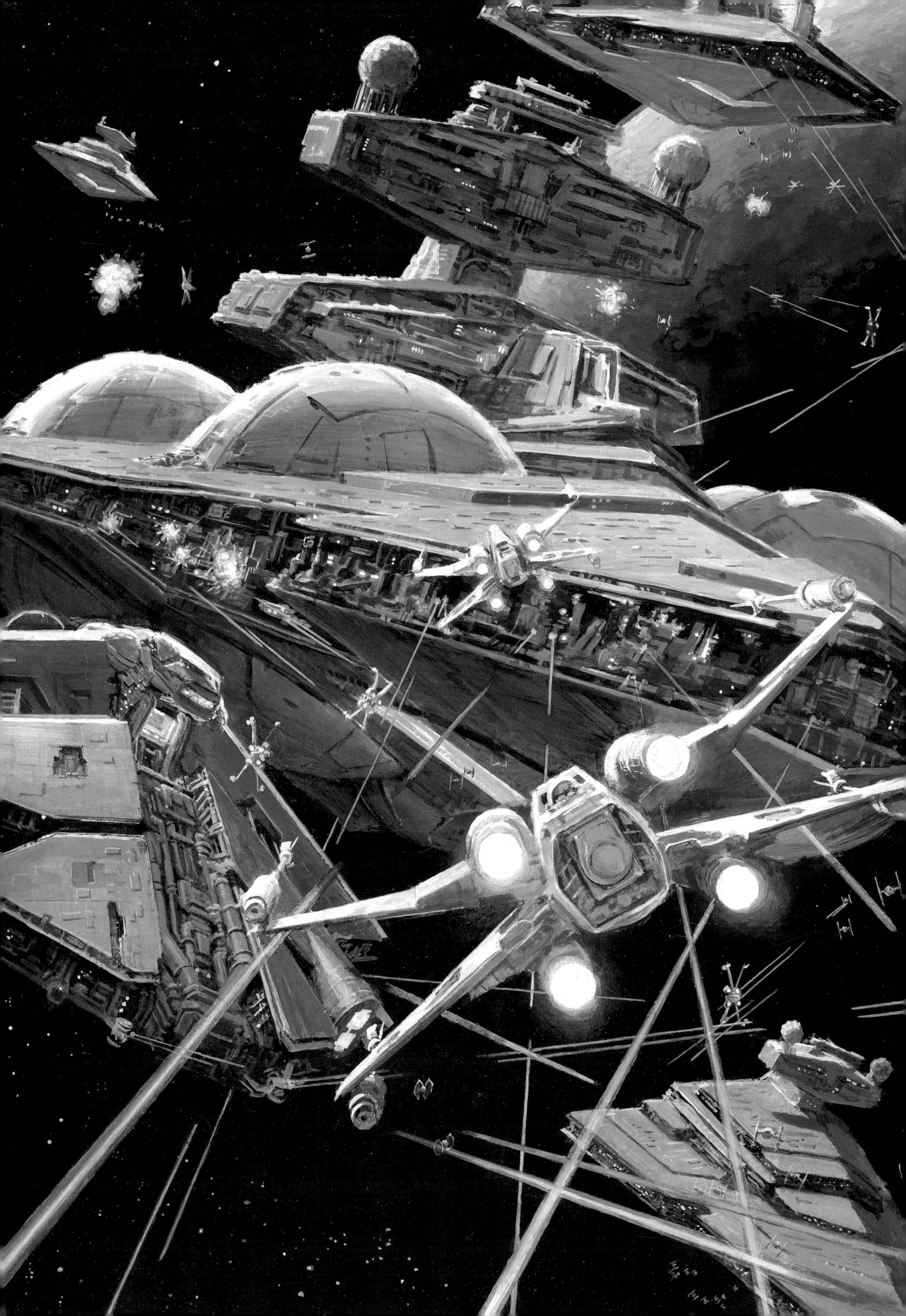

And they were met by the Empire's finest. Here we see Baron Fel, ace of aces.

Previous: art by John Nadeau. X-Wing: Rogue Squadron *#32 (1998). This page: art by Tim Bradstreet and Grant Goleash.* X-Wing: Rogue Squadron—Blood and Honor *(1999).*

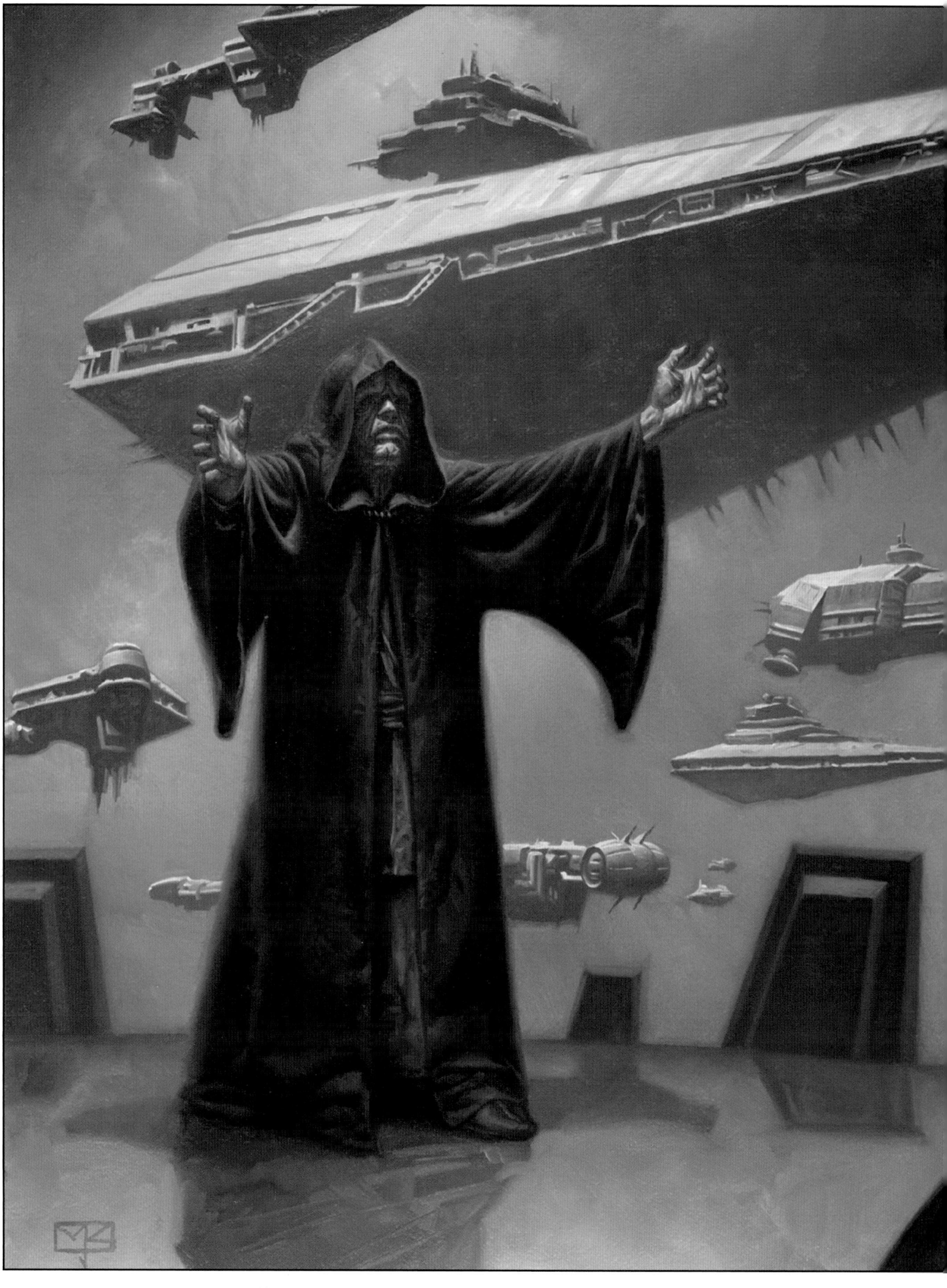

Then, after six years (*Star Wars* time) of continued strife, things suddenly got worse for the New Republic. Emperor Palpatine was resurrected in a clone body, and in an effort to defeat him, Luke Skywalker nearly succumbed to the dark side.

Art by Mark Zug. Dark Empire I, *third edition (2003).*

The Dark Empire saga marked Dark Horse's entrance into the Expanded Universe. A decade and a half later, it remains the best-selling graphic novel in the *Star Wars* line.

Dark Empire spawned two sequels, *Dark Empire II* and *Empire's End*, which well and truly put a cap on Palpatine's reign.

Art by Tsuneo Sanda. Dark Empire II, *second edition (2006).*

153

The Empire, like nature, abhors a vacuum, and it wasn't long before a number of different individuals lay claim to the vacant Imperial throne. But one man, Kir Kanos, the last of the betrayed and murdered Imperial guards, defied all of them . . .

. . . even to the point of siding (briefly) with the forces of the New Republic.

Meanwhile, Luke Skywalker undertook the rebuilding of the Jedi order. Establishing an academy in the old Rebel base on Yavin 4, Luke began training a new generation of Jedi Knights to become, as he put it, "the paladins of the New Republic."

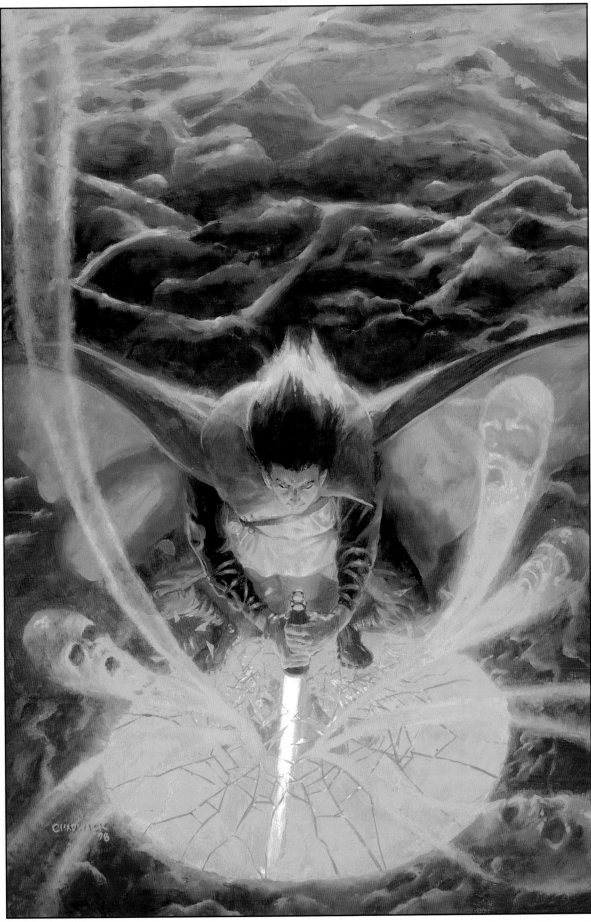

And, though some of Luke's students would go on to fulfill his expectations, the Jedi—and indeed, the entire galaxy—was about to face an unexpected threat . . .

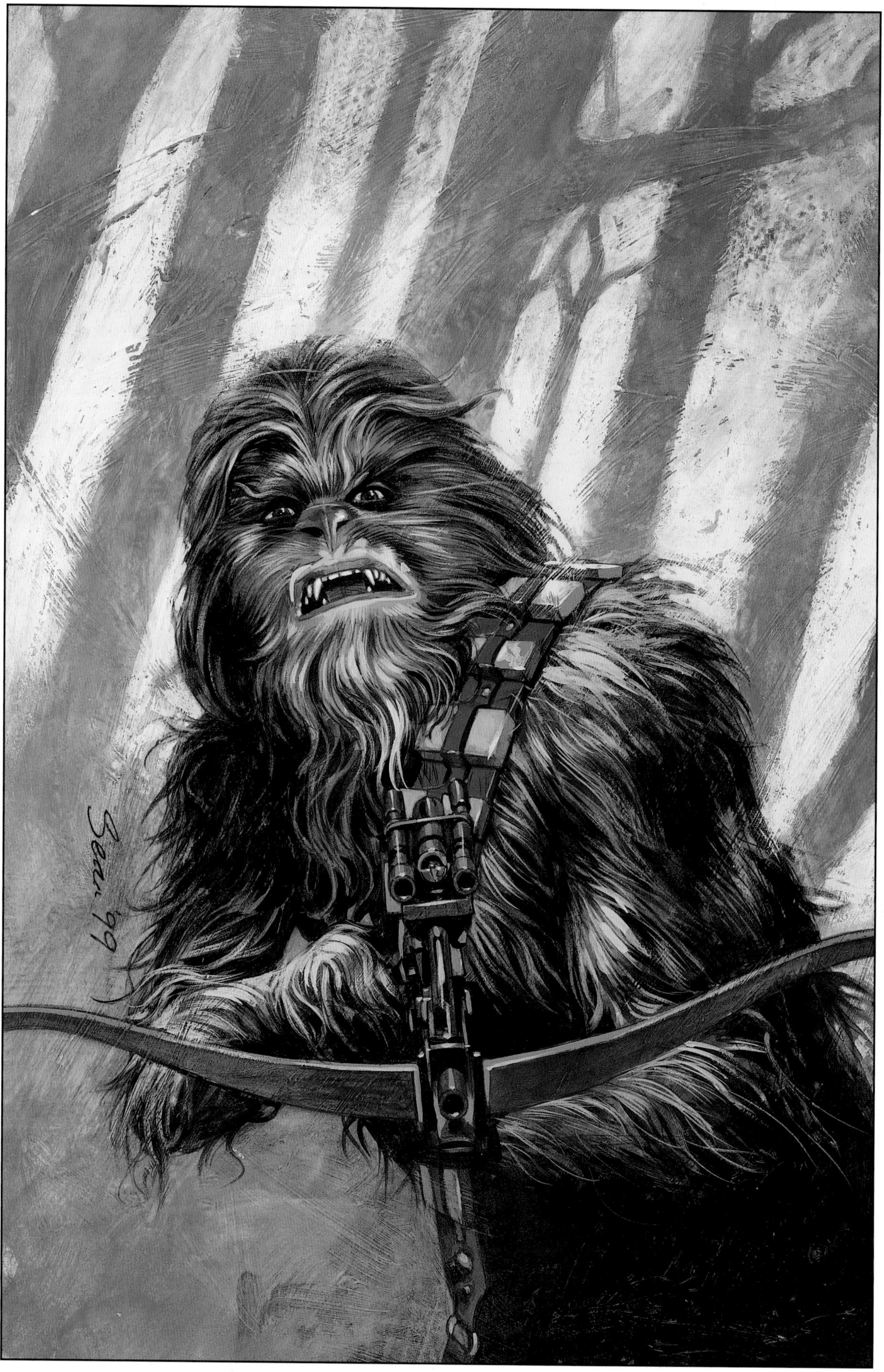
Sean '99

. . . one that would take the life of one of the most beloved members of Luke's extended family. The alien Yuuzhan Vong were responsible for Chewbacca's death, but the mark they left on the galaxy went so much deeper . . .

 Art by Sean Phillips. Chewbacca *#1 (2000) and the collection of the same name (2001).*

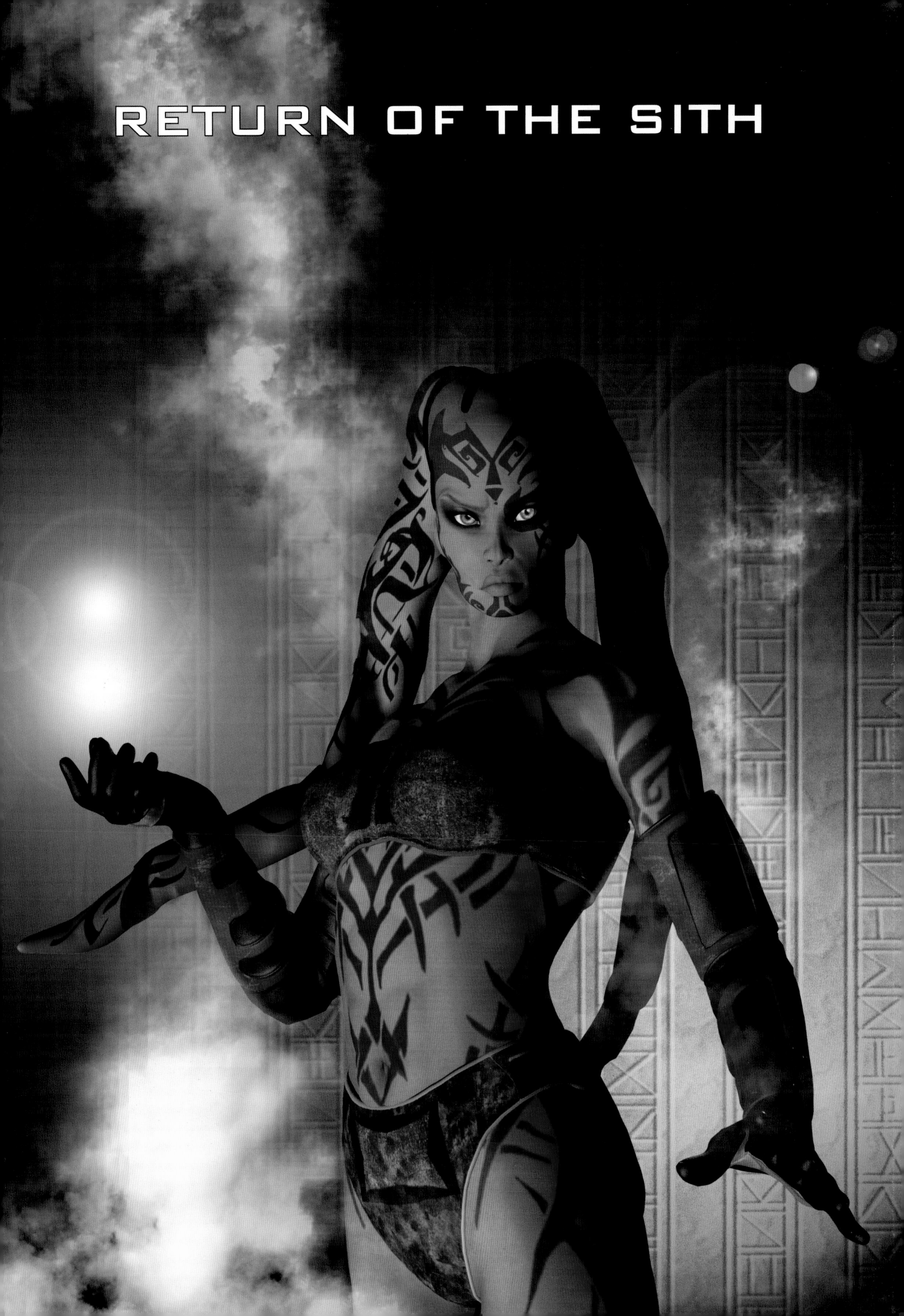
RETURN OF THE SITH

SUDDENLY, ONE HUNDRED YEARS LATER . . .

In 2006, as part of Dark Horse's twentieth anniversary revamp of our entire *Star Wars* line, we took a gamble and introduced *Legacy*. Readers were dropped into brand new continuity set one hundred years after anything they knew (and 137 years after the Battle of Yavin). The invasion by the Yuuzhan Vong—and their subsequent defeat—had changed the balance of power in the galaxy. The Jedi order, seeking to undo some of the damage caused by the Yuuzhan Vong, convinced Yuuzhan Vong Shapers to restore some planets' ecosystems.

Previous page: art by Jan Duursema. Legacy #0 (2006).

This was the moment for which a hidden—but resurgent—Sith order had been waiting. The Sith secretly sabotaged the restoration attempts, making it look like a Jedi plot. The Galactic Alliance (what the former New Republic had become), siding with the Jedi, found itself once again at war with the Empire.

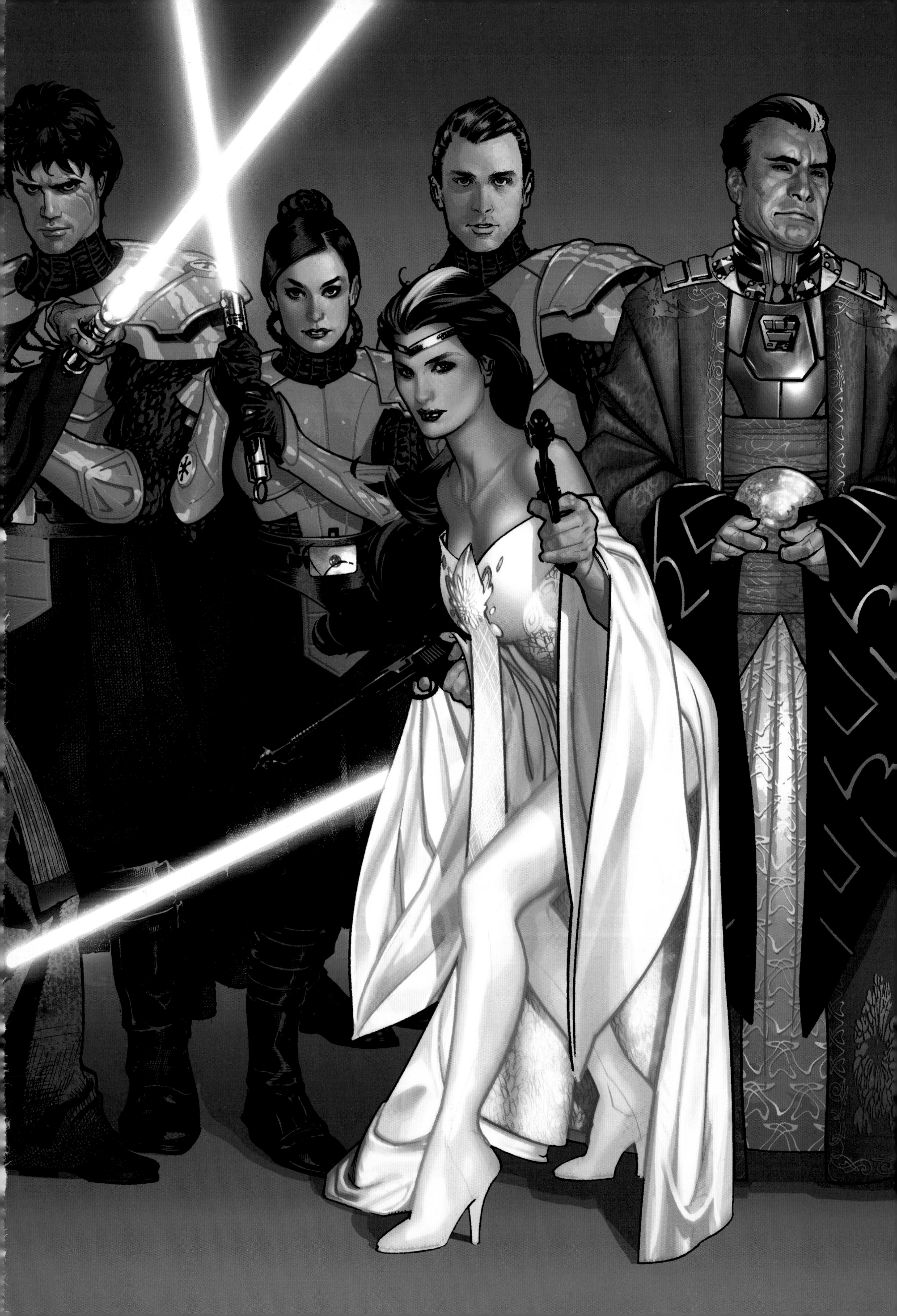

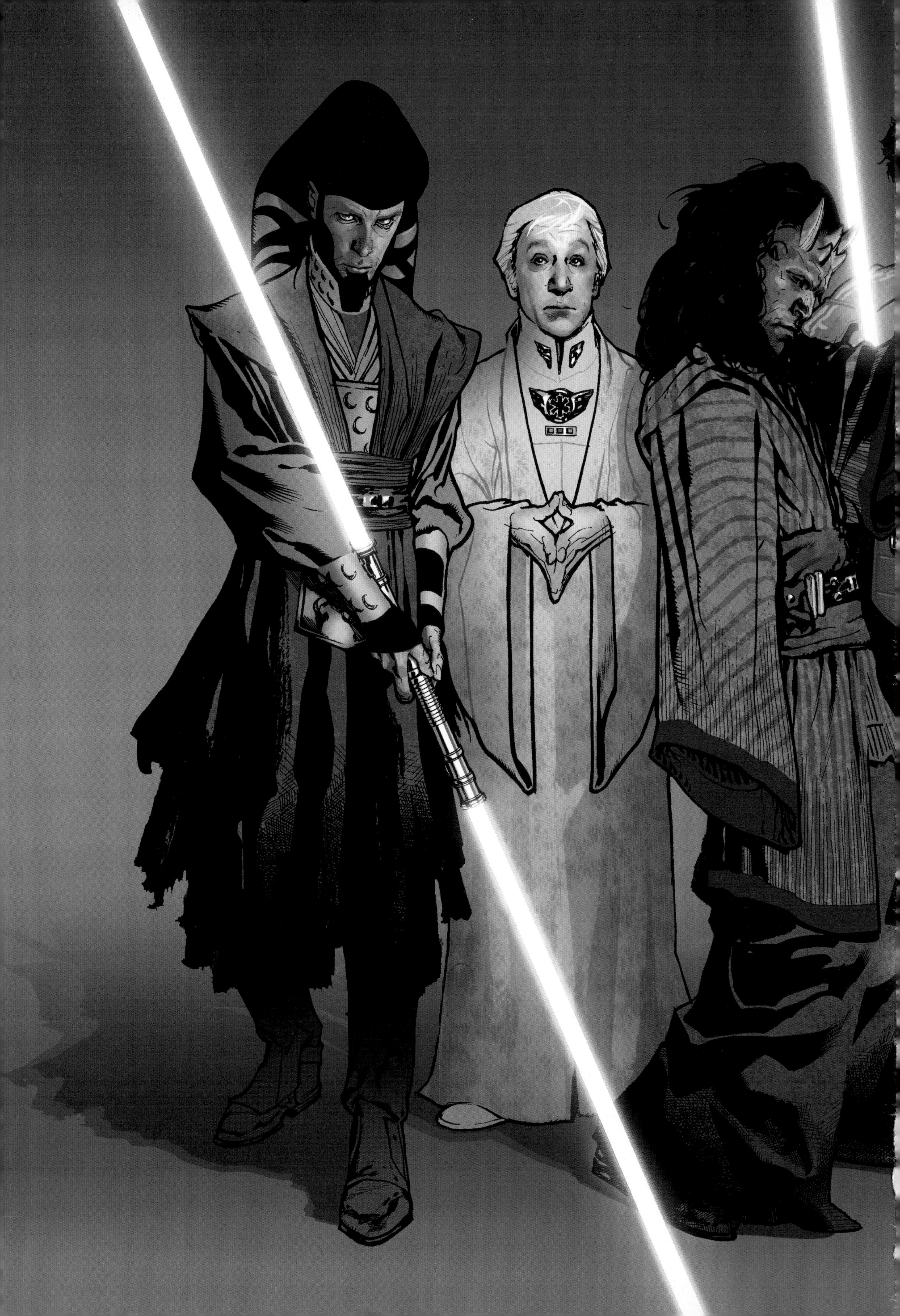

But war also raged within the Empire. Aided by two ambitious Moffs, Morlish Veed and Nyna Calixte, the Sith, under the command of the mysterious Darth Krayt, took the Imperial throne and attempted to assassinate Emperor Roan Fel. Unfortunately for them, Fel was warned of the trap and the Sith only succeeded in killing his double.

This page: script by John Ostrander, art by Adam DeKraker, colored by Brad Anderson, lettering by Michael David Thomas. Legacy #8 *(2007). Overleaf: art by Adam Hughes. Cover montage from* Legacy #1-3, 5-7 *(2006-2007).*

The Sith were more successful in their attack on the Jedi academy on Ossus. Backed by their stormtrooper allies, the Sith killed many Jedi—including Kol Skywalker, then head of the Jedi Council. Kol's son Cade witnessed his death.

Script by John Ostrander, pencils by Jan Duursema, inks by Dan Parsons, colored by Brad Anderson, lettering by Michael David Thomas. Legacy #1 (2006) and Legacy *Volume 1 (2007).*

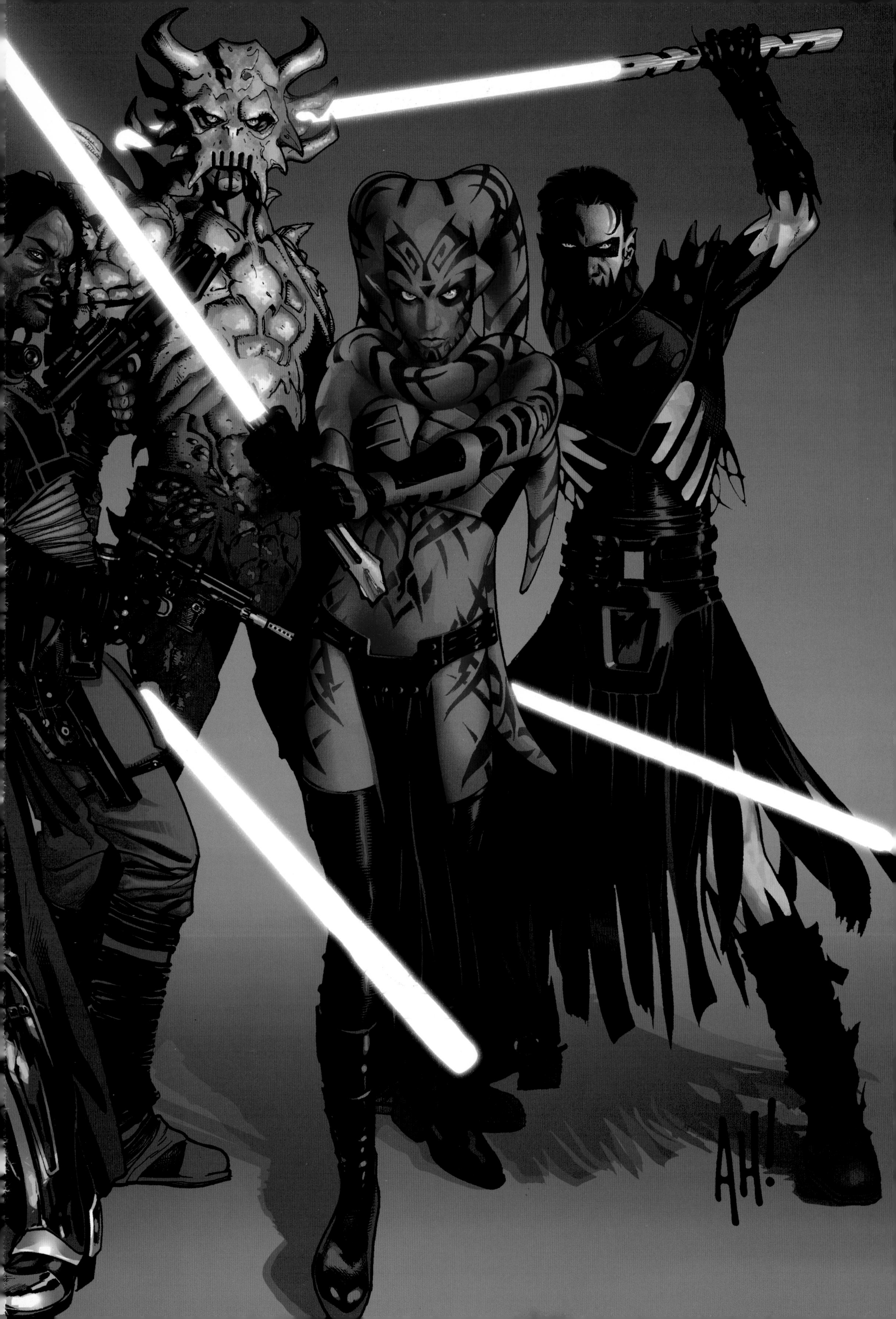
AH!

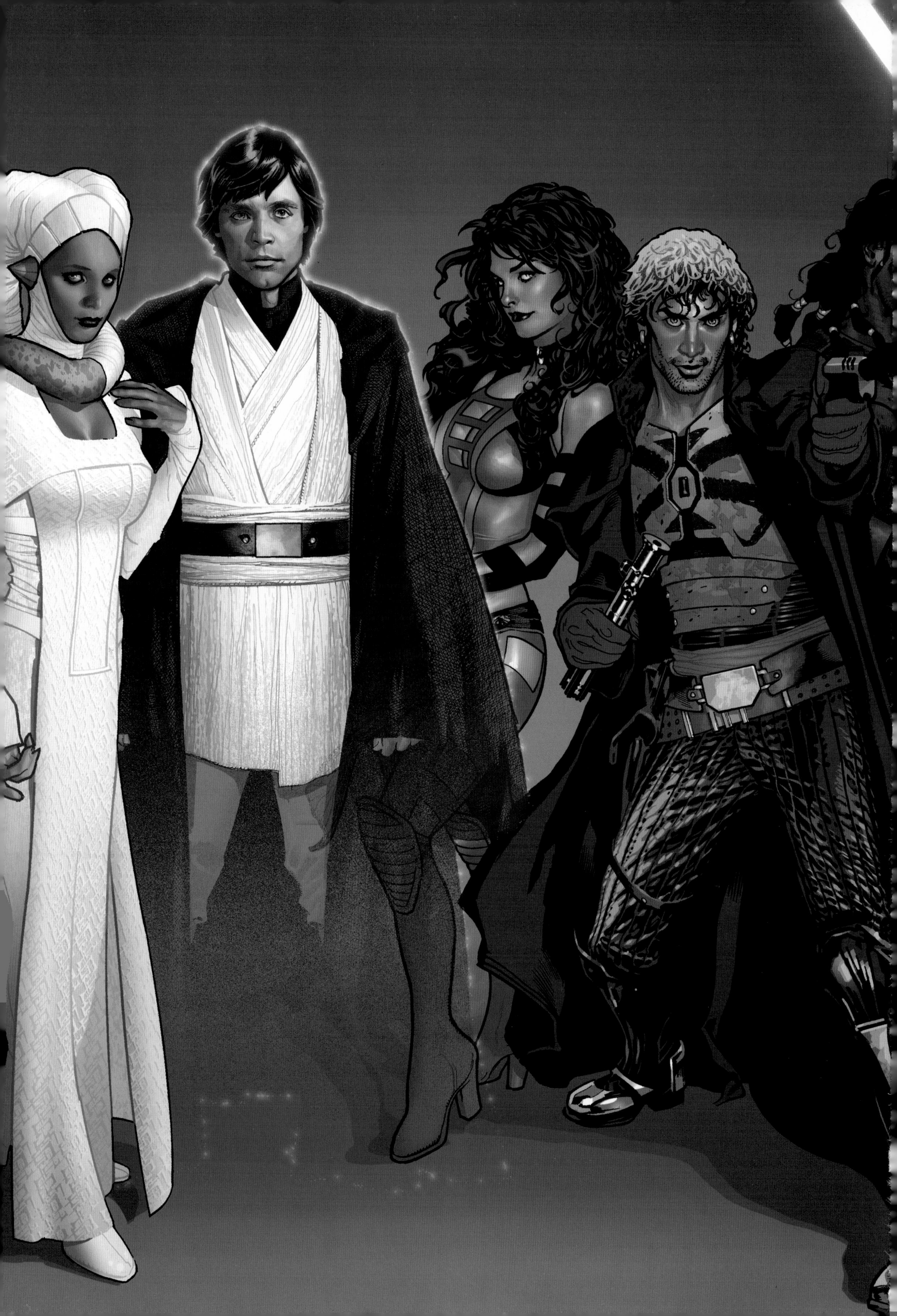

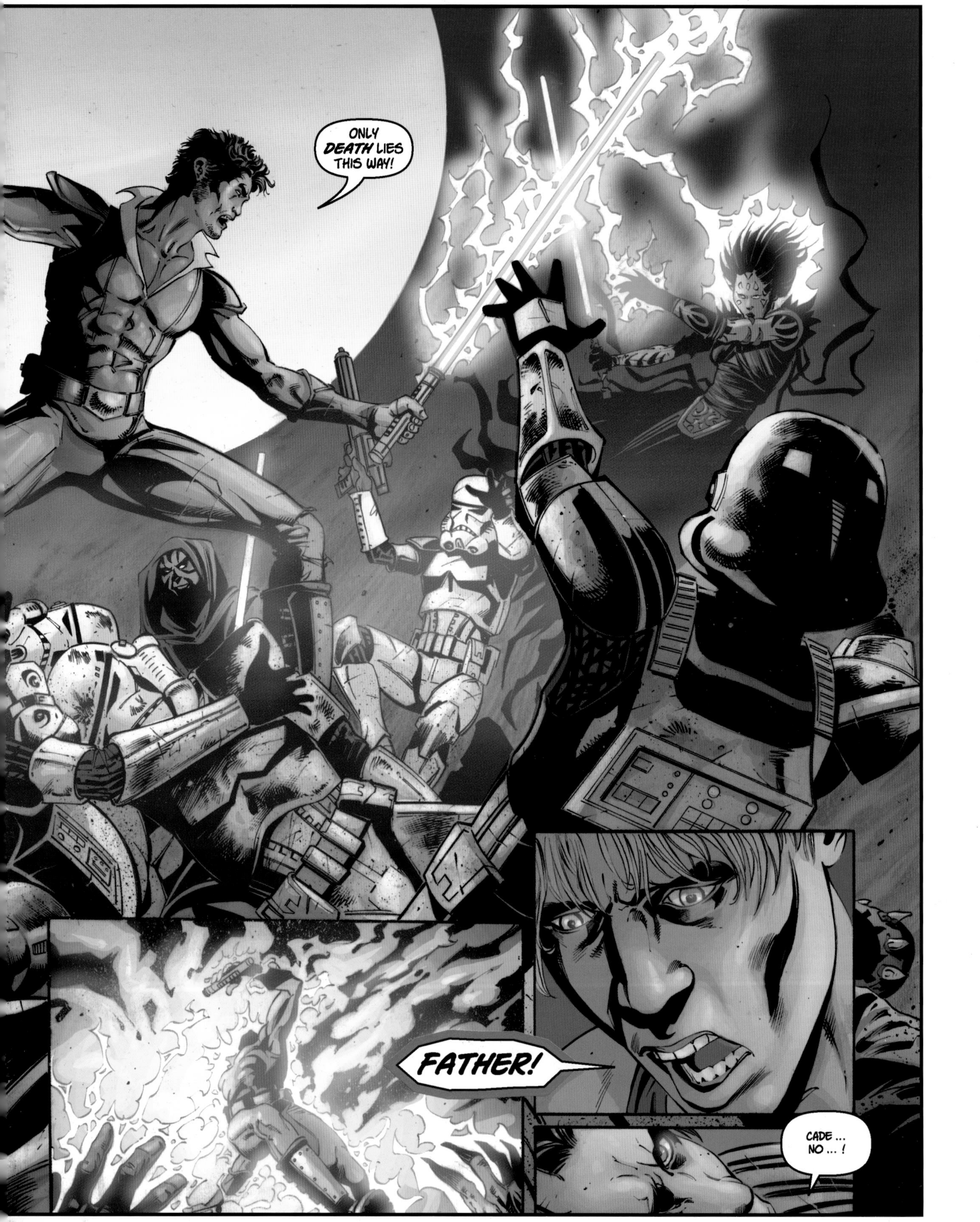
ONLY DEATH LIES THIS WAY!
FATHER!
CADE ... NO ... !

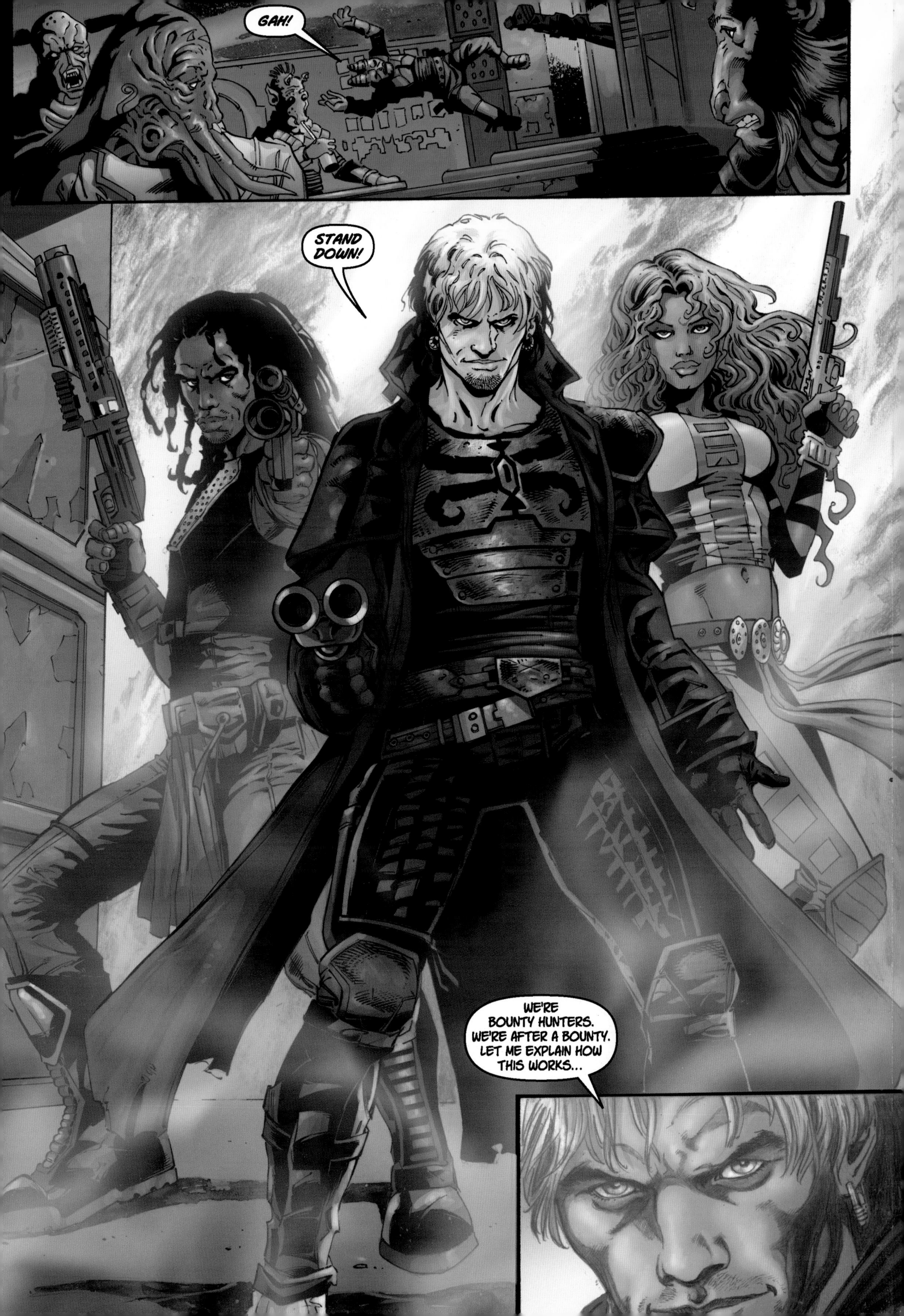
GAH!
STAND DOWN!
WE'RE BOUNTY HUNTERS. WE'RE AFTER A BOUNTY. LET ME EXPLAIN HOW THIS WORKS...

Seeing his father murdered and the Jedi scattered had a profound effect on Cade Skywalker. He spent the next seven years running from his own heritage. He crewed for a pirate, then started his own bounty-hunting operation with partners Jeriah Syn and Deliah Blue. But there was one figure from his past he just couldn't shake . . .

Previous page: script by John Ostrander, pencils by Jan Duursema, inks by Dan Parsons, colored by Brad Anderson, lettering by Michael David Thomas. Legacy #2 *(2006)* *and* Legacy Volume 1 *(2007). This page: same team.* Legacy #3 *(2006).*

And once word got out that a Skywalker had survived the massacre on Ossus, *everybody* was looking for him—the Jedi, the Sith, and the scheming Moffs Veed and Calixte. It is eventually revealed that Moff Calixte has her own reasons for seeking Cade . . .

What transpired during the century between the end of Del Rey's *Legacy of the Force* novels and the beginning of the comics series *Legacy*? What is the origin of the enigmatic Darth Krayt and his legion of Sith? Will Cade Skywalker accept, or reject, his legacy? These are mysteries that only time can answer. But for now, it looks as though Cade has broken his vow to never again pick up a lightsaber!

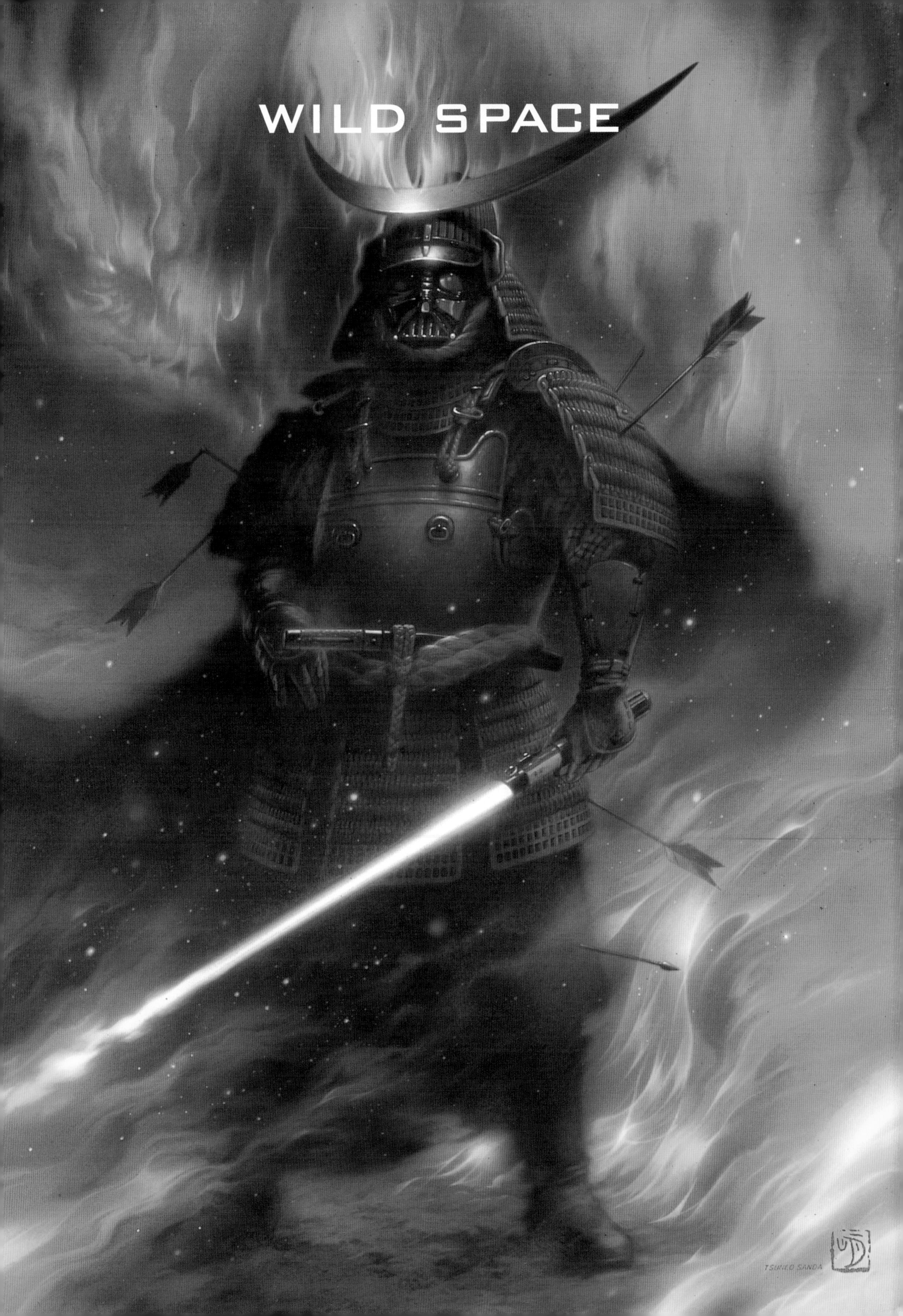
WILD SPACE
TSUNEO SANDA

INFINITIES AND BEYOND

"Infinities" is the designation given by Lucasfilm to *Star Wars* stories that couldn't possibly happen—or at least couldn't happen exactly as depicted. Sometimes it's just a matter of the humor or the action being amped up to a ridiculous degree. Other times events in a tale fly in the face of established continuity, defy the laws of time and space, have characters behave other than themselves, or all three. Whatever the case, Dark Horse has produced a number of stories which fit this category.

Previous page: art by Tsuneo Sanda. Star Wars Tales *Volume 1 (2002).*

Usually these forays beyond the realm of canon are purely for the sake of humor, as with the Tag and Bink stories. Tag and Bink are two hapless Rebel soldiers who infiltrate the Imperial forces—much to their regret.

But they can also allow writers and artists to play with situations which could never occur in "real life," like this duel between Darths Vader and Maul . . .

Script by Ron Marz, pencils by Rick Leonardi, inks by Terry Austin, colored by Raul Trevino, lettering by Steve Dutro.

. . . or Indiana Jones and Short Round discovering Han Solo's remains within the crashed *Millennium Falcon*, guarded by a Wookiee "sasquatch."

The Infinities venue even allowed real people (like Dark Horse editor Dave Land) to interact with *Star Wars* characters. And vice versa.

Script by Dave Land, art by Lucas Marangon, lettering by Steve Dutro. Star Wars Tales #13 (2002).

The original trilogy of films also received the Infinities treatment. In the Infinities version of *A New Hope*, Luke's proton torpedoes malfunctioned and detonated early, failed to destroy the Death Star, and . . .

Script by Chris Warner, pencils by Drew Johnson, inks by Ray Snyder, colored by Dave McCaig, lettering by Steve Dutro. Infinities: A New Hope #1 (2001), *collected in* Infinities: A New Hope *(2002).*

. . . set up an entirely different chain of events.

Art by Tony Harris, colored by Chris Blythe. Infinities: A New Hope #2 *(2001) and in the collection (2002).*

Put into the *Infinities* blender, *The Empire Strikes Back* was altered when Luke died after being mauled by the wampa in the ice cave . . .

Script by Dave Land, pencils by Davidé Fabbri, inks by Christian Dalla Vecchia, colored by Dan Jackson, lettering by Steve Dutro. Infinities: The Empire Strikes Back #1 *(2002), collected in 2003.*

. . . leading to a very different confrontation with Vader in the end. And, in *Infinties: Return of the Jedi* . . . well, you get the idea.

Script by Dave Land, pencils by Davidé Fabbri, inks by Christian Dalla Vecchia, colored by Dan Jackson, lettering by Steve Dutro. Infinities: The Empire Strikes Back #4 (2002), collected in 2003. Opposite: art by Rodolfo Migliari. Infinities: Return of the Jedi #4 (2004) and the collection in the same year.

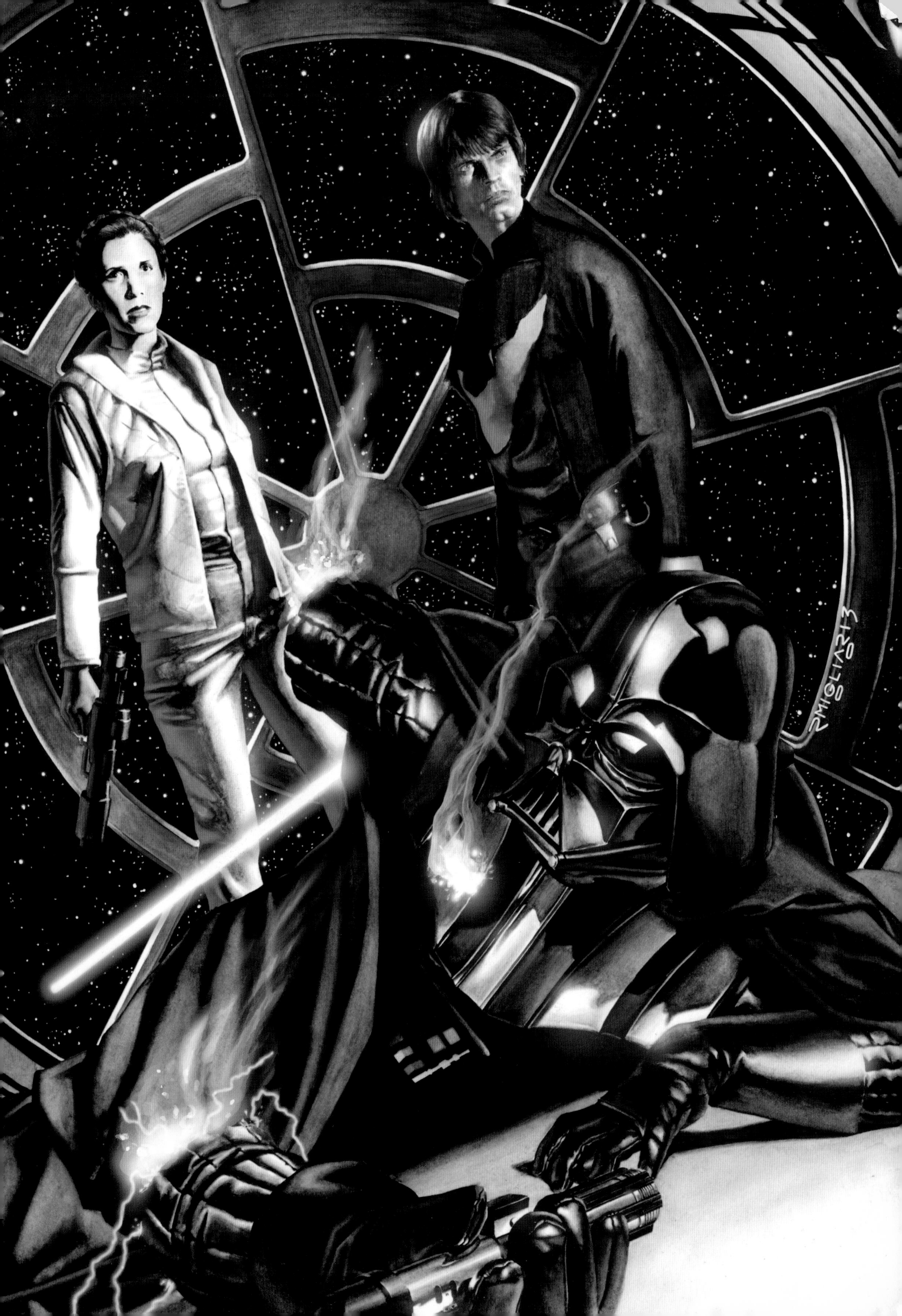

Of course, not everything that is not-exactly-canon fell under the Infinities banner. For instance, stories told in the style of the *Clone Wars* cartoons were allowed a bit of leeway.

But *nobody* was allowed more leeway than famed cartoonist Sergio Aragonés who, in a mere twenty-two pages reduced the *Star Wars* galaxy to rubble. (Sergio had previously given both the Marvel and DC comic-book universes the same treatment.)

Art by Sergio Aragonés, colored by Dave McCaig. Sergio Aragonés Stomps Star Wars *(2000).*

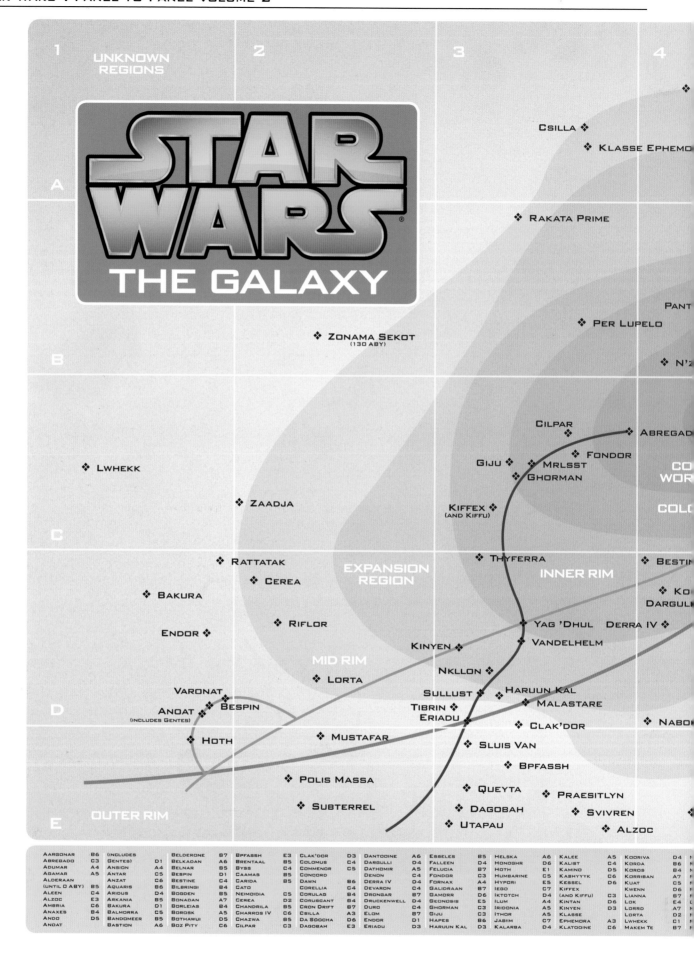

Location	Grid		Location	Grid		Location	Grid		Location	Grid		Location	Grid		Location	Grid		Location	Grid		Location	Grid		Location	Grid
Aargonar	B6		(includes			Belderone	B7		Bpfassh	E3		Clak'dor	D3		Dantooine	A6		Esseles	B5		Helska	A6		Kalee	A5		Kooriva	D4
Abregado	C3		Gentes)	D1		Belkadan	A6		Brentaal	B5		Colomus	C4		Dargulli	D4		Falleen	D4		Honoghr	D6		Kalist	C4		Korda	B6
Adumar	A4		Ansion	A4		Belnar	B5		Byss	C4		Commenor	C5		Dathomir	A5		Felucia	B7		Hoth	E1		Kamino	D5		Koros	B4
Agamar	A5		Antar	C5		Bespin	D1		Caamas	B5		Concord			Denon	C4		Fondor	C3		Humbarine	C5		Kashyyyk	C5		Korriban	A7
Alderaan			Anzat	C6		Bestine	C4		Carida	B5		Dawn	B6		Derra IV	D4		Fornax	A4		Hypori	E5		Kessel	D6		Kuat	C5
(until 0 ABY)	B5		Aquaris	B6		Bilbringi	B4		Cato			Corellia	C4		Devaron	C4		Galidraan	B7		Iego	C7		Kiffex			Kwenn	D6
Aleen	C4		Aridus	D4		Bogden	D4		Cerea	D2		Corulag	B4		Druckenwell	D4		Gamorr	D6		Iktotch	D4		(and Kiffu)	C3		Lianna	B7
Alzoc	E3		Arkania	B5		Bonadan	A7		Chandrila	B5		Coruscant	B4		Duro	C4		Geonosis	E5		Ilum	A4		Kintan	D6		Lok	E4
Ambria	C6		Bakura	D1		Borleias	B4		Charros IV	C6		Cron Drift	B7		Elom	B7		Ghorman	C3		Iridonia	A5		Kinyen	D3		Lorrd	A7
Anaxes	B4		Balmorra	C5		Borosk	A5		Chazwa	B5		Csilla	A3		Endor	D1		Giju	C3		Ithor	A5		Klasse			Lorta	D2
Ando	D5		Bandomeer	B5		Bothawui	D5		Cilpar	C3		Dagobah	E3		Eriadu	D3		Hapes	B6		Jabiim	C7		Ephemora	A3		Lwhekk	C1
Anoat			Bastion	A6		Boz Pity	C6											Haruun Kal	D3		Kalarba	D4		Klatooine	C6		Makem Te	B7

MAJOR HYPERSPACE ROUTES

CORELLIAN RUN
CORELLIAN TRADE SPINE
HYDIAN WAY
PERLEMIAN TRADE ROUTE
RIMMA TRADE ROUTE

WORK FROM THE FOLLOWING ARTISTS APPEARS ON THE NINE-PANEL GRIDS ON PAGES 8, 20, 38, 50, 70, 92, 116, 160, AND 174:

Brad Anderson, colors

Curtis Arnold, inks

Michael Atiyeh, colors

Terry Austin, inks

Brandon Badeaux, art

Batt, colors

David Jacob Beckett, inks

Joel Benjamin, colors

Ryan Benjamin, pencils

Bill Black, inks

Patrick Blaine, art

Chris Blythe, colors

Jim Campbell, colors

Dario Carrasco, Jr., pencils

Brian Ching, art

Chris Chuckry, colors

Joe Corroney, art

Saleem Crawford, inks

Christian Dalla Vecchia, inks

Rodolfo Damaggio, pencils

Adam DeKraker, art

Digital Chameleon, colors

Terry Dodson, pencils

Dave Dorman, art

Jan Duursema, pencils

Lee Evandon, colors

Davidé Fabbri, pencils

The Fillbach Brothers, art

Travel Foreman, art

Tomás Giorello, pencils

Wil Glass, colors

Chris Gossett, art

Paul Gulacy, pencils

Mark G. Heike, inks

Heroic Age, colors

Brian Horton, art

Dan Jackson, colors

Drew Johnson, pencils

Robert Jones, inks

Rafael Kayanan, art

Jason Keith, colors

Cam Kennedy, art

Igor Kordey, art

Ray Kryssing, inks

Fabio Laguna, inks

Paul Lee, art

Rick Leonardi, pencils

Mark Lipka, inks

Tom Luth, colors

Tom Lyle, inks

Rick Magyar, inks

James Mason, colors

Dave McCaig, art, colors

Adriana Melo, art

Tony Millionaire, art

Makoto Nakatsuka, art

Dave Nestelle, colors

Kevin Nowlan, inks

Dan Parsons, pencils

Ronda Pattison, colors

Kilian Plunkett, art

Pamela Rambo, colors

Al Rio, pencils

David Roach, art

Luke Ross, art

P. Craig Russell, inks

Stan Sakai, art

James Sinclair, colors

Ray Snyder, inks

Chris Sprouse, pencils

Dave Stewart, colors

Sno Cone Studios, colors

Timothy II, art

Francisco Ruiz Velasco, art

Russell Walks, art

Joe Wayne, colors

Dustin Weaver, art

Joe Weems, inks

Doug Wheatley, art

Al Williamson, inks

Colin Wilson, art

Anthony Winn, pencils

Walden Wong, inks

A frontispiece by artist Tsuneo Sanda graced our first volume of *Star Wars: Panel to Panel*, showing a multitude of characters from the *Star Wars* films. For this volume, we commissioned Mr. Sanda to create a companion piece with characters primarily from the Expanded Universe, most of whom debuted in comic books. Here is a handy key to those characters, creatures, and machines, as well as the comics series in which they first appeared. Main characters and devices from the films are listed in bold-face.

1. X-wing
2. Pellaeon-class Imperial Star Destroyer (*Legacy*)
3. The *Uhumelé* (*Dark Times*)
4. The *Mynock* (*Legacy*)
5. Scythe-class Galactic Alliance Battle Cruiser (*Legacy*)
6. Predator-class Imperial Fighter (*Legacy*)
7. World Devastator (*Dark Empire*)
8. The *Last Resort* (*Knights of the Old Republic*)
9. Nu-class Imperial Shuttle (*Legacy*)
10. A-wing
11. a mamien (*Empire*)
12. Biggs Darklighter (*Empire*)
13. Kyp Durron (*Jedi Academy*)
14. Wedge Antilles (*X-Wing: Rogue Squadron*)
15. Nera Dantels (*Empire*)
16. A'sharad Hett (*Star Wars/Republic*)
17. Del Moomo (*Knights of the Old Republic*)
18. Dob Moomo (*Knights of the Old Republic*)
19. Q'Anilia (*Knights of the Old Republic*)
20. Lucien Draay (*Knights of the Old Republic*)
21. Kirana Ti (*Jedi Academy*)
22. Morlish Veed (*Legacy*)
23. Aurra Sing (*Star Wars/Republic*)
24. Clone Wars-era AT-AT (*Republic*)
25. Dorsk 82 (*Jedi Academy*)
26. Nyna Calixte (*Legacy*)
27. Roan Fel (*Legacy*)

28. An'ya Kuro, AKA Dark Woman (*Star Wars/Republic*)
29. Streen (*Jedi Academy*)
30. Ganner Krieg (*Legacy*)
31. Marasiah Fel (*Legacy*)
32. Ulic Qel-Droma (*Tales of the Jedi*)
33. Sigel Dare (*Legacy*)
34. a rancor
35. Asajj Ventress (*Republic*)
36. Cal Qel-Droma (*Tales of the Jedi*)
37. Nomi Sunrider (*Tales of the Jedi*)
38. Micah Giiett (*Jedi Council*)
39. a Yinchorri warrior (*Jedi Council*)
40. K'Kruhk (*Jedi Council*)
41. BoShek (*Empire*)
42. Rasha Bex (*Empire*)
43. Quinlan Vos (*Star Wars/Republic*)
44. Khaleen Hentz (*Republic*)
45. Vilmarh Grahrk (*Star Wars/Republic*)
46. Aayla Secura (*Star Wars/Republic*)
47. Zayne Carrick (*Knights of the Old Republic*)
48. Camper (*Knights of the Old Republic*)
49. T1-LB (*Knights of the Old Republic*)
50. Jarael (*Knights of the Old Republic*)
51. Marn Hierogryph (*Knights of the Old Republic*)
52. Rav (*Legacy*)
53. Deliah Blue (*Legacy*)
54. Cade Skywalker (*Legacy*)
55. Jariah Syn (*Legacy*)
56. Kenix Kil (*Crimson Empire II*)
57. Schurk-Heren (*Dark Times*)

58. ARC trooper (*Republic*)
59. Mezgraf (*Dark Times*)
60. Sadeet (*Crimson Empire*)
61. Kir Kanos (*Crimson Empire*)
62. Ko Vakier (*Dark Times*)
63. Carnor Jax (*Crimson Empire*)
64. Mirith Sinn (*Crimson Empire*)
65. Sora Bulq (*Jedi: Mace Windu*)
66. a clone trooper riding a motmot (*Republic*)
67. Anakin Skywalker
68. T'ra Saa (*Republic*)
69. Tholme (*Star Wars/Republic*)
70. Meekerdin-maa, AKA Ratty (*Dark Times*)
71. Sian Jeisel (*Republic*)
72. Gauer (*Empire*)
73. Moff Trachta (*Empire*)
74. Darth Talon (*Legacy*)
75. Darth Krayt (*Legacy*)
76. Darth Nil (*Legacy*)
77. Obi-Wan Kenobi
78. Darth Wyyrlok (*Legacy*)
79. Queen Jool (*Legacy*)
80. 4/NG (*Crimson Empire II*)
81. Grappa the Hutt (*Crimson Empire II*)
82. Dass Jennir (*Dark Times*)
83. Amanin warrior (*Empire*)
84. Deena Shan (*Empire*)
85. Raze (*Rebellion*)
86. Janek Sunber (*Empire*)

87. Bomo Greenbark (*Dark Times*)
88. Wyl Tarson (*Rebellion*)
89. Sagoro Autem (*Republic*)
90. Isaru Omin (*Republic*)
91. a whuffa (*Star Wars*)
92. Astraal Vao (*Legacy*)
93. Shado Vao (*Legacy*)
94. R2-D2
95. C-3PO
96. Wolf Sazen (*Legacy*)
97. Konrad Rus (*Legacy*)
98. Mouse (*Empire*)
99. Mace Windu
100. Durge (*Republic*)
101. an acklay
102. Mara Jade (*Mara Jade*)
103. an Imperial Guard (*Crimson Empire*)
104. Darth Vader
105. Luke Skywalker (circa *Legacy*)
106. Han Solo
107. Leia Organa Solo
108. Exar Kun (*Tales of the Jedi*)
109. Naga Sadow (*Tales of the Jedi*)
110. Rohlan Dyre (*Knights of the Old Republic*)

Key by Ryan Hill

STAR WARS GRAPHIC NOVEL TIMELINE (IN YEARS)

The Golden Age of the Sith—5,000 BSW4
Fall of the Sith Empire—5,000 BSW4
Knights of the Old Republic—4,000 BSW4
The Freedon Nadd Uprising—3,998 BSW4
Dark Lords of the Sith—3,997 BSW4
Sith War—3,996 BSW4
Redemption—3,986 BSW4
Commencement—3,964 BSW4
Jedi vs. Sith—1000 BSW4
Stark Hyperspace War—44 BSW4
Qui-Gon & Obi-Wan—38-37 BSW4
Jedi Council—33.5 BSW4
Prelude to Rebellion—33 BSW4
Darth Maul—33 BSW4
Republic Volumes 1-9—32-19 BSW4
Star Wars: Episode I—The Phantom Menace—32 BSW4
Outlander—31 BSW4
Emissaries to Malastare—31 BSW4
Twilight—30 BSW4
Jedi Quest—28 BSW4
Jango Fett—27 BSW4
Zam Wesell—27 BSW4
Starfighter—24 BSW4
Star Wars: Episode II—Attack of the Clones—22 BSW4
Clone Wars—22-19 BSW4
General Grievous—20 BSW4
Star Wars: Episode III—Revenge of the Sith—19 BSW4
Dark Times—19 BSW4
Droids—5 BSW4
Jabba the Hutt: Art of the Deal—5 BSW4
Boba Fett: Enemy of the Empire—3 BSW4
Classic Star Wars: Han Solo at Stars' End—2 BSW4
Underworld—1 BSW4
Star Wars: Episode IV—A New Hope—SW4
Empire Volumes 1-7—0 ASW4
Rebellion—0 ASW4
Vader's Quest—0+ ASW4
Classic Star Wars: The Early Adventures—0+ ASW4
River of Chaos—0+ ASW4
Classic Star Wars—0-3 ASW4
Shadow Stalker—0-3 ASW4
Splinter of the Mind's Eye—2 ASW4
Star Wars: Episode V—The Empire Strikes Back—3 ASW4
Tales From Mos Eisley—3 ASW4
Shadows of the Empire—3+ ASW4
Star Wars: Episode VI—Return of the Jedi—4 ASW4
Jabba the Hutt: The Jabba Tape—4 ASW4
Mara Jade—4 ASW4
Shadows of the Empire—Evolution—4 ASW4
Classic Star Wars: The Vandelhelm Mission—4+ ASW4
X-Wing Rogue Squadron—4+ ASW4
Boba Fett: Twin Engines of Destruction—5 ASW4
Heir to the Empire—9 ASW4
Dark Force Rising—9 ASW4
The Last Command—9 ASW4
Dark Empire—10+ ASW4
Boba Fett: Death, Lies, and Treachery—10+ ASW4
Boba Fett: Agent of Doom—10+ ASW4
Empire's End—11 ASW4
Crimson Empire—11+ ASW4
Jedi Academy: Leviathan—12 ASW4
Union—20 ASW4
Chewbacca—25 ASW4
Legacy—137 ASW4

Old Republic Era
25,000 – 1000 years before
Star Wars: A New Hope

Rise of the Empire Era
1000 – 0 years before
Star Wars: A New Hope

Rebellion Era
0 – 5 years after
Star Wars: A New Hope

New Republic Era
5 – 25 years after
Star Wars: A New Hope

New Jedi Order Era
25+ years after
Star Wars: A New Hope

Legacy Era
130+ years after
Star Wars: A New Hope

Infinities
Does not apply to timeline

Sergio Aragones Stomps Star Wars
Star Wars Tales
Infinities
Tag and Bink
Star Wars Visionaries

BSW4 = before *Episode IV: A New Hope*. ASW4 = after *Episode IV: A New Hope*.

191